Sandford and Phare force us to consider deep ethical questions regarding our relationship with fresh – questions that we must face but have yet to face in this country. *Ethical Water* takes us well beyond a new conception of an old problem; it leaves us with the foundations of a new water ethic that is, at its core, anchored in the simple fact that each and every drop of the water we humans use is water we share with all life on Earth.

—Tony Maas, Freshwater Program Director,
World Wildlife Fund Canada

In this clearly written little book, Sandford and Phare argue convincingly that Canada urgently needs a national water policy, and that it would best be based on a water ethic similar to that of First Nations. I agree.

—Dr. David Schindler, Killam Memorial Professor of Ecology,
University of Alberta

Ethical Water is a crisp, compelling argument about why Canadians need to urgently make some very tough decisions about how we have traditionally viewed the role of water in our society. Rather than just ringing the alarm bell, Robert and Merrell-Ann provide a thoughtful ethical lens to help guide the transition from where we are today to the establishment of a world-class, sustainable approach to caring for the one thing that matters most: water.

—Don Lowry, President & CEO, EPCOR

Ethical Water should be required reading for serving politicians at the municipal, provincial/territorial and federal levels. There are things we have to do, while there is still time.

—The Honourable J. Michael Miltenberger,
Deputy Premier of the Northwest Territories

Ethical Water

LEARNING TO VALUE WHAT
MATTERS MOST

*Robert William Sandford and
Merrell-Ann S. Phare*

RMB
Victoria Vancouver Calgary

Rocky Mountain Books
www.rmbooks.com

Library and Archives Canada Cataloguing in Publication

Sandford, Robert W.
    Ethical water : learning to value what matters
most / Robert William Sandford, Merrell-Ann S. Phare.

Includes bibliographical references.
Issued also in electronic format. (ISBN 978-1-926855-71-4)
ISBN 978-1-926855-70-7

    1. Water-supply. 2. Water conservation. 3. Water resources development.
4. Fresh water. I. Phare, Merrell-Ann, 1965– II. Title.

HD1691.S26 2011   333.91   C2011-903307-0

Printed and bound in Canada

Rocky Mountain Books acknowledges the financial support for its publishing program from the Government of Canada through the Canada Book Fund (CBF) and the province of British Columbia through the British Columbia Arts Council and the Book Publishing Tax Credit.

 Canadian Heritage Patrimoine canadien   Canada Council for the Arts Conseil des Arts du Canada

 BRITISH COLUMBIA ARTS COUNCIL

The interior pages of this book have been produced on 100% post-consumer recycled paper, processed chlorine free and printed with vegetable-based dyes.

 MIX Paper from responsible sources FSC® C016245

Contents

*As the gulf between those with sufficient
water and those without deepens as a source
of grievance, inequity and conflict, the
new politics of scarcity in mankind's most
indispensable resource is becoming an
increasingly pivotal fulcrum in shaping
the history and environmental destiny
of the twenty-first century.*

— *Steven Solomon,*
Water: The Epic Struggle for
Wealth, Power, and Civilization

Toward a New Canadian Water Ethic

It is well known that our blue globe is by definition a water world. It is also recognized that 97 per cent of the water on this planet is salty, leaving only 3 per cent of it fresh enough to sustain terrestrial life. Of that 3 per cent, much of the world's fresh water is bound in ice or is inaccessible to us because it lies so deep beneath the surface of the Earth. During any given hundred-year period, water will spend 98 years in the ocean, 20 months in ice, two weeks in lakes and rivers, and one week in the atmosphere. This is what we have to work with. The same four-thousandths of 1 per cent of the Earth's total water sustains us today as has sustained every other civilization since the beginning of time.

As Steven Solomon observes in his book *Water: The Epic Struggle for Wealth, Power, and Civilization*, the long record of the rise and fall of hydraulic societies throughout history demonstrates that an abundance of water is important and necessary for the development of a strong, independent sovereign state, but it does not assure it. Abundance of water in itself is no guarantee of economic prosperity or long-term sustainability for a nation, an empire or a civilization.

History is littered with the artifacts of societies that declined simply because they could not overcome the effects of local resource depletion, could not manage the impacts of population expansions that accompanied their own initial success. A hallmark of the failed societies of the past is a growing dependence on water-engineering cleverness that defies natural design. We try to manage water better but we do it through increasingly costly and extraordinary means. What history tells us is that what is required for survival and sustainability is the prudent use of water in the broadest range of changing environmental, economic, social and political circumstances.

Of all the hydraulic civilizations, ours is the most extensive, in both reach and impact. By 2000 we had constructed some 45,000 large dams that in combination with the hundreds of thousands of smaller structures quadrupled water storage for human purposes in only 40 years. Depending on the season, three to six times the amount of water that exists at any given moment in all the world's rivers is now stored behind giant dams. But no one examined or was able to predict the cumulative global-scale effect uncoordinated dam building, irrigation diversions and the related impacts of deforestation would have on the timing and extent of water availability. The waters of some 17 major river systems around the world no longer make it to the sea. To these impacts add unexpected rapid increases in temperatures, and belatedly we realize our own potential to alter our planet's water cycle.

For better or worse, human activity is affecting our planet's hydrology. Our presence and our actions have altered the very composition of the atmosphere in which our precipitation forms and from which our rain falls. Our actions have also altered how much land cover exists to capture, store, purify and release water that falls from the sky. We are now affecting rainfall patterns and how much water flows in rivers and whether our rivers make it to the sea. Though it is hard to comprehend how, we have even altered the acidity of our oceans.

The same ecosystem depletions and limitations that brought down earlier empires all over the world are now appearing on a global scale, threatening all of us, rich and poor. We have added a new twist, however: new and complex forms of persistent pollutants that threaten almost every water source on the planet, thereby reducing the amount of water available for use.

The growing awareness of our effects on how water acts in the world presents us with a fundamental crisis of values that may mark a juncture in the narrative not just of the human journey but of the story of life on Earth. Despite this, there continues to be widespread failure to change our behaviour. In our current way of thinking, water is seen as an entitlement of rapidly expanding human populations that grow ever more wealthy by ignoring not only the moral requirement for water allocation to all, but also the pressing water needs of the surrounding natural landscapes, which are valued only to the extent that they may harbour resources useful for further development.

As Steven Solomon notes, experts around the world are arguing that water is the most grossly misgoverned, misallocated and profligately wasted natural resource on the planet. This cannot continue without risking the collapse of the very systems we depend on, not just for survival but for meaning and value in our lives.

As Peter Brown and Jeremy Schmidt point out in their anthology *Water Ethics: Foundational Readings for Students and Professionals*, we face a stark choice. We can choose to live in "a denuded, simplified, dangerous and quite possibly dying world" or we can create and act upon a new narrative, one in which the decisions we make about water use – the ends to which we put our knowledge and technological sophistication – are founded on broad cultural, religious and moral values that respect the water needs of the non-human life community. What we need as a foundation for such a narrative is a new water ethic. If we wish to achieve any meaningful degree of sustainability, we must create that ethic now.

PART ONE

Canada: Where We Have Been and Where We Are Now

For the nearly 500 years that have passed since Jacques Cartier sailed up the St. Lawrence, that most historic of Canadian rivers, water has made us wealthy. As is often the custom with wealthy people, we have, over time, lost touch with the source and true nature of our wealth. Ours is one of the few cultures that have ever had the luxury of being able to take water for granted. But now, in a nation that is not even a century and a half old, things have definitely changed. We have discovered to our dismay that the qualities that make water so diversely valuable to us are the same qualities that easily allow it to become contaminated, polluted and lost to further use. As our population has grown, and the range of our agricultural, industrial and recreational activities has multiplied, we have strained the waters those activities depend on. At the same time, we have come up against the limits of what we know and can predict about how much water we will have in the future. In a single generation – one human lifetime – we have gone from a country that took great pride in the fact that one could drink from almost any river, sparkling stream or lake in the country, to a nation seriously concerned about water quality and availability now and in the future.

Though we cling tenaciously to the image we have created of ourselves as a nation of wild rivers and infinitely available clean water, we are undone by the reality that is so clearly presenting itself to us. Our place is not the only place where this is occurring, of course. Canada is a microcosm of what is happening to water all over the world. Even the remaining uninhabited parts of Canada and their original sources of clean, fresh water now contain pollutants that were created thousands of kilometres away. Many of the densely inhabited southern areas of our country are beginning to face water quality and availability issues. Some places are already in crisis. From this it is easy to see which way history is flowing with respect to this most important of all natural systems. Problems associated with water in Canada are here to stay. It is time for water to re-enter Canadian consciousness. It is time for a new Canadian water ethic.

In pursuing this ideal, however, we should not discount the possibility that we may discover that the foundations of the water ethic Canadians may wish to adopt have been in our possession for centuries but remain hidden in plain sight as a result of our gradual loss of direct and immediate emotional connection to the rivers, lakes and streams that historically have defined us as a people.

DEFINING A WATER ETHIC

In the simplest of terms, an ethic can be defined as a set of moral principles concerning human conduct in the context of our relationships with one another and with the rest of the world. As human populations and their demands grow globally, and as landscape change and climate warming put inadequacies of contemporary frameworks of management into relief, ethical considerations are poised to rise to prominence in water management decision-making.

Ethics deals with disagreements about how we ought to deal with the problems we face in the world. In chapter 1 of the anthology *Water Ethics*, co-editor Jeremy Schmidt characterizes these disagreements as arising in three fundamental domains. The first revolves around claims related to the actual state and fate of our current water supplies. Contention arises around what we know about the condition of these systems and what we actually mean when we make a claim to "adequate" supplies and quality. The second fundamental disagreement revolves around how social relationships should be ordered with respect to the competing claims of economics, basic human rights to water, the rights of ecosystems to their own integrity, and the rights of people to property and prosperity. And third, all of these considerations have to be balanced against water's significance to people of often widely differing values, beliefs or cultures.

Schmidt observes that, at present, global

policy discourse on water ethics pits disparate views about the relevance of water to human existence against one another. Matters as diverse as the intrinsic value of water – the economic pricing of water – are in competition with equity of supply, in terms of assuring adequate availability to everyone who needs water and to intergenerational needs for assured water security, with all of those issues then being deliberated as against nature's own needs for water. There is a growing number of observers who believe this debate is complicated at the moment by the fact that it is being undertaken on behalf of and often without the knowledge of most Canadians by experts who claim to represent Canadians' interests even when that may not strictly be true.

The reason discourse has been confined to expert circles is that most Canadians have no idea of the water ethic they have consciously or unconsciously subscribed to over the past century – if any – and fewer still have realized the need for creating a different one. Most Canadians don't know where they are coming from with respect to water, and therefore do not know where we are going. If we want to manage water sustainably, that has to change.

CANADA'S FOUNDING WATER ETHIC

Canada has possessed a water ethic for thousands of years. The origins of Canada's founding water ethic begin with the indigenous peoples of North America. The fundamental principles concerning appropriate human conduct with respect to water in both its physical and spiritual manifestations were clearly defined in these societies and were passed from generation to generation through moral lessons which were then affirmed in practice. Three fundamental principles remain at the heart of traditional First Nations water ethics even today.

First, fundamental to the traditional ways of many indigenous peoples is that the use of water by humans is governed by a relationship of mutual responsibility. Water looks after us, so we look after water. All actions taken must ensure that this reciprocal responsibility is honoured. The Western notion of rights to water does not come into play in traditional indigenous peoples' water ethics. The Western idea implies a one-way relationship that is out of balance and ultimately destructive and unsustainable: I take and water gives. Relationships with all aspects of the world, being based on the need to maintain reciprocity and mutual respect between themselves and humans, do not abide this unbalanced approach.

In our Western system, water use is generally constrained only by external forces such as limits on taking and using water within the terms and conditions of a licence. Internal limits, however – such as knowing that your use of water creates and is circumscribed by a responsibility to ensure that the waters continue to exist in such a state and flow as to purify themselves and to nourish and sustain all life – are secondary considerations, if they exist at all, in our current economic and legal models. Yet these ideas are at the very core of indigenous peoples' traditional relationships with lands and waters.

Second, a commonality of most or all indigenous traditional cultures is that they view the Earth as a living entity comprised of spiritual beings in a multitude of forms including plants, animals, rocks, air and water. Because water exists everywhere in and around us, from the cellular right up to the planetary scale, and we are wholly dependent upon it for life, we have a more direct relationship with water than with any other substance on Earth except perhaps air (which in turn is seen as being one with water). Water washes us and the Earth clean. It sustains life. It plays a significant ceremonial and symbolic role in the lives of indigenous peoples, just as it does in most of the world's religions. We know water and water knows us. This is why it is that even if raised in a city, most people feel generally peaceful, contemplative, grounded and joyful when in the presence of natural bodies of water. Indigenous peoples often say that to sever the spiritual connection that humans inherently have to water is devastating to both ourselves and to water. This is a fundamental tenet of the relationship, in essence the partnership, that humans have with water. It is a relationship that is not only physical but also spiritual and emotional. Humans not only use water, we *feel* water.

First Nations traditional principles and Aboriginal ways of being regarding water embrace this human connection with water and the reciprocal responsibilities that go with it. While we might not realize it – in fact, most aspects of modern life are designed so that we do not notice it at all – most of us, even many indigenous peoples, today sense a pervasive, "non-point-source" lack of connection to water that cannot be restored through occasional trips to the beach.

Regrettably, the water ethic that has emerged in Canada since European settlement has proven to be antithetical to the founding water ethic established here by First Nations. To relate to water – especially in our economic and legal dealings – as a resource rather than as a precious physical and spiritual partner in life, is, in the opinion of many indigenous peoples, to make it very convenient to avoid responsibility for the destruction of water.

Third, in many indigenous cultures it is women who are the holders of responsibility for the waters. Traditionally they have had a critical role in maintaining both the responsibility for – and the spiritual relationship with – water. For contemporary indigenous women, concerns about ecosystem use, climate change and other issues are not as neatly compartmentalized as they are in the broader societal context in which First Nations struggle to maintain their values. As women in these cultures are charged with caring for, protecting and providing water in all situations, they are expected to be involved in and ultimately to govern decision-making related to waters and the environment.

First Nations women continue to define their responsibility to water as they go and as these duties grow. They constantly remind one another by example that their responsibility begins with remembering that, as human beings, they must ensure the continuance of the larger community of life whenever they take one of that community's members for their own personal use, be it a tree, a fish or a living water molecule. Many indigenous women feel that because they have been taught this, it no longer matters as much which race or gender they belong to. They will build community with anyone who wishes to join them, and they will join with others who also feel this way. To them, this is their responsibility as women and as persons. No amount of generosity, it appears, will make this an easy task.

This role is increasingly difficult to discharge because of pressures that have handicapped not only indigenous women but all indigenous peoples. In Canada these pressures include Indian Act-imposed forms of governance which limit women's traditional methods of involvement in decision-making; the historical outlawing of spiritual practices; the loss of cultural and spiritual traditions due to residential schools; and the impacts of extreme poverty, which threaten to elevate typical forms of economic development such as mining, hydroelectricity, forestry and other resource-intensive activities to the status of imperatives regardless of the accompanying environmental and social costs. However, according to indigenous scholar David Newhouse in a 2010 speech at Dalhousie University, "the key modern Aboriginal desire is to use indigenous ideas and theories as key informing principles and foundations of everyday life." When Newhouse talks about "everyday life" he means the lives of all of us, of all Canadians.

THE SYMBOLIC NATURE OF
FIRST NATIONS WATER ISSUES

Because they have been so staunchly opposed, central elements of the founding water ethic in Canada as established by the First Peoples have over the last three centuries been extensively eroded by the practices of others. Today, indigenous peoples continue to face huge challenges in trying to protect their lands and waters from environmental degradation. They find themselves in the midst of a process of decolonizing, and in many instances they face serious economic, health, social, cultural and legal challenges to restoring their communities to their pre-Contact vibrancy and self-sufficiency.

Canadian indigenous scholar Leanne Simpson has spoken about an elder who told her that it took 500 years to get into this situation and it will likely take 500 more to get out of it. Many First Nations assert that patience, determination and long-term, unwavering focus are needed in the face of the complexity of today's challenges. Non-indigenous Canadians with concerns about the state and fate of the global environment are now reluctantly beginning to accept that the same expanded timeframes and unwavering intergenerational commitment that First Nations have long accepted are what the rest of the world will have to match if broader societal change is to result in any meaningful form of sustainability.

Many indigenous nations in Canada are in negotiations with other governments to restore legal recognition of title to their territorial lands and waters, the connection to which they never relinquished. Others are directing suing for recognition of their water rights. The core of the opposition to First Nations legal challenges regarding water is, in many circles, an incorrect belief that indigenous peoples no longer have legal rights to the waters in and on their territories. This belief is manifested through regular exclusion of indigenous peoples from water-related decision-making processes of federal and provincial governments. Although indigenous peoples are sometimes involved in "consultation"-type processes where they are presented with the opportunity to provide their perspectives and thoughts, this type of involvement does not constitute a decision-making role. Alberta's Water for Life and Ontario's Source Water Protection Planning Framework are two such consultation-type processes that do not constitute consultation to the extent now required by federal law, nor do they represent the kinds of partnership-oriented processes that are necessary both to allow for indigenous water rights to be equitably realized and to meaningfully address the serious water issues we already face.

More and more non-Aboriginal Canadians are beginning to realize they are in the same situation as indigenous peoples in that they never consciously chose to relinquish their relationships with water. They were not – nor are they being – adequately consulted on water issues. They did not consciously agree to let others divert or pollute their water. Neither was it their idea to turn water into a market commodity or to deny water to ecosystems that need it. Yet, because they are a product of their own industrialized society – of choices made before and for them – many non-Aboriginal Canadians are finding themselves in the same struggle as First Nations: the struggle to reconnect, restore, recognize and feel their relationship to the world around them. It is not just the water belonging to the indigenous peoples that is being compromised; it is everyone's water.

The problems associated with First Nations water security are increasingly being seen as heavily symbolic. Despite billions spent on water security on First Nations reserves, these problems are not going away. In recent years, the numbers of drinking water advisories have been slowly creeping upward. Some reserves have been subject to drinking water advisories for as long as 18 years. This means there are children on those reserves who have grown up knowing no other way of securing safe tap water other than by boiling it. But these problems are not likely to remain confined to remote reserves. No matter where you live in Canada, issues related to water quality and quantity are coming to a location near you.

THE SURPRISING SCALE OF CANADA'S WATER ISSUES

The issues related to water in Canada are much more serious and of greater persistence than most Canadians imagine. The alarming state of our groundwater was put into relief by a 2009 Council of Canadian Academies report which demonstrated that aquifer contamination is widespread throughout the country. We are even polluting aquifers we share with our US neighbours.

Agricultural water use is also becoming an issue all across Canada. This is because contemporary industrial-scale food production practices inevitably result in reduced return flows to nature of poor-quality water which already-diminished and often water-starved natural systems no longer have the capacity to purify. As a result, thousands of Canadian lakes and watercourses are now suffering from various degrees of the nutrient and pesticide loading that leads to eutrophication. We are not adequately maintaining our urban and rural water infrastructure and so it is increasingly vulnerable to more frequent and intense extreme-weather events such as floods, storms and tornadoes. Growing amounts of endocrine-altering substances and contaminants of emerging concern are finding their way into our water supplies. The management of water systems in the context of continued oil sands development in the Athabasca River basin is already in dispute and represents an area of elevated conflict that casts Canada in a poor light on the international stage. It has been observed that what previously threatened only First Nations, now – or ultimately – threatens all of us.

Indifference to such concerns is increasingly held to be economically, socially and environmentally unacceptable. Now we sense that the choices we are making are morally unacceptable as well. It has been argued that water is our most misgoverned, most inefficiently and inequitably allocated and most profligately wasted natural bounty. Clearly there is no small measure of urgency, and perhaps even great opportunity, in changing that.

STARTING AGAIN FROM THE BEGINNING

Upon consciously beginning the journey of reconnection to natural ecological processes, people all over the country are learning from indigenous peoples' examples that sustainability begins, and likely ends, with water. In searching for and wanting to build community with water, Canadians are rediscovering that it is impossible to ignore – and indeed desirable and necessary to build connections with – other species and entities that live on, in, through, with or near water. In this context, it is impossible not to recognize our responsibilities to them. Sustainability demands recognition of these connections.

While most non-indigenous people in Canada may not be ready to accept that reconnecting to the moral, ethical and spiritual significance of water is essential to the long-term sustainability of our society, a growing number of concerned Canadians inside and outside of established environmental circles maintain that the only way to effect real change may be to return to a fundamental belief in the value and necessity of indigenous peoples asserting their rights regarding their lands and waters. To these people this has to be the starting place, at least, for the creation of a new Canadian water ethic, because any other approach would disavow the history and connection of indigenous peoples to the lands and waters all across Canada.

THE UPHILL PUSH TOWARD MORE
EFFECTIVE WATER GOVERNANCE

Water policy discussions are these days increasingly urgent and focused. There seems to be awareness that without comprehensive and immediate action, our water woes will only increase and at an accelerating rate. Likely this awareness stems from a number of factors, such as:

~ water-related impacts of climate change being felt strongly in certain regions of the country (extreme drought in southern Alberta, for example);

~ government deregulation in the area of environmental protection (such as changes to the Navigable Waters Protection Act that eliminate consideration of impacts on smaller rivers, and changes to Fisheries Act regulations that allow for the sacrifice of small lakes for use as storage ponds for toxic mine tailings); and

~ water-related program cuts as a result of cyclical economic recession and government priorities on deficit reduction (such as ongoing reduction of scientific expertise within the federal government).

Whatever the reason, discussions about water increasingly focus on the creation of effective federal water policy as a critical implement in the solutions toolbox. A federal water policy is seen as a unifying principle that governs the federal family and its decision-making and that provides binding national standards in areas such as drinking water and minimum in-stream flow requirements to protect aquatic ecosystems. Effective federal water management is seen as a means of maintaining peace and securing order as an expression of good government.

The expanding discussion also embraces the harmonization of federal, provincial and territorial water management oversight and regulation. Opinion in the water community also appears to be solidifying around the realization that cooperative and coordinated definition and discharge of the roles and responsibilities of the provinces, municipalities and indigenous peoples' governments are also critical for effective governance of water.

This is excellent progress. A growing consensus is being reached regarding the ultimate goal of most water policy development efforts: effective governance resulting in efficient, sustainable water use.

But although participants in the discussion offer various prescriptions and alternative pathways to solve the water problems we face, there is also emerging a general agreement that despite progress in some areas, water governance as it currently exists is simply not effective. Evidence of this is cited by the website "The Water Chronicles," which reports on the current status of drinking water advisories in effect in Canada (www.water.ca/map-graphic .asp): as of June 2011 there were some 1,100. To experts, such numbers suggest a problem of massive scale, one not restricted to certain areas (such as rural communities) or to certain groups (such as First Nations) or to certain aspects of water decision-making (such as management of water treatment plants). What this suggests is that the problem is systemic and related to the effectiveness of governance. In the water policy arena, unfortunately, we are not yet certain what "effective governance" looks like. We are still at the "well, we'll know it when we see it" stage. We may not know it even if we do see it, however, unless we make a conscious effort to determine how existing governance structures might be reformed so as to make safer, more efficient and sustainable water management possible.

What we mean by "efficient water use" (or phrases expressing a similar goal that encompasses the desire to define and set limits on who gets to use which water and for which purpose) is even more troubling. What "sustainability" actually means is also problematic. Though vigorous, the debate appears to be dividing Canadians rather than getting us where we want to go.

To some, the question that matters most in this debate relates to the paramount importance of ensuring adequate water for ecosystems. Others believe the focus should be on water conservation efforts by humans. Still others are worried that the impacts of a changing climate will be so severe that emphasis must be placed on better understanding these impacts and acting accordingly and soon (or now). For some, the question is purely one of governance: who is included in making decisions and how decisions are made. This last group holds that if the appropriate structure is built, governance will create the right result regarding water policy outcomes. Others believe that none of these actions will get us where we want to go, because they deal with symptoms rather than the central problem. They have a point. We will continue to stumble forward without vision unless we first ask ourselves the most important question of all: what kind of future are we trying to create? Without an answer to this question as a baseline, any future outcome will be deemed a success or failure by interests able to capitalize on any given political moment. In others words, nothing will change.

PART TWO

The Emerging Global Future: Why Canada Needs a New Water Ethic

For the first time in history, as Steven Solomon points out in *Water: The Epic Struggle for Wealth, Power and Civilization*, the fundamental economic and political rules governing water are beginning to be transformed by market ideology and by the power of the marketplace itself. With the spectre of water scarcity appearing widely in the world, the relentless laws of supply and demand have mobilized the market economy's expansive, profit-seeking aspirations with the aim of turning water into an object of market interest and activity. Water is already a $400-billion-a-year industry and growing rapidly. The prospect of a profit bonanza has set off a worldwide scramble to control water and infrastructure and to turn water into a commodity to be traded in the same way as oil, timber, copper or pork bellies.

Market interest in water represents a turning point in the future of liberal democracy in that it demands a different balance between economy and environment than has existed to date. In *The Wealth of Nations*, Adam Smith made famous the description of the market's "invisible hand" that miraculously transforms individual self-interest and competitive pursuit of profit into the wholesome maximization of wealth creation for the entire society. Yet, as evidenced by the deteriorating state of our global environment, the market has glaringly failed to evolve any corresponding "invisible green hand" that automatically reflects the cost of depleting natural resources and maintaining the overall environment qualities upon which an orderly, prosperous society ultimately depends for its stability and sustainability. Green GDP calculations suggest, for example, that environmental damage is cancelling out most if not all of China's much-touted economic miracle. It has been estimated that as many as 750,000 people die in China each year from water and air pollution, and yet this "externality" is not identified as a cost associated with the country's "economic miracle."

The challenge for liberal democracies posed by market interest in the global water crisis is that water isn't at all like a "natural resource." While it may be painful to substitute alternative energy sources for oil, for example, such substitutes do exist. But there is no substitute for water. As Steven Solomon points out, water is much more than the new oil. Water is an essential element in everything we do and make. We literally cannot live without it. More than any other substance on Earth, water is utterly indispensable. By virtue of its scarcity, irreplaceability and broader utility, water demands to be treated differently than "natural resources." The blind, invisible hand of the market, being limited in its sensory capacities, can't see that the democracy we need is a water democracy where all of earth's inhabitants have their voice.

There are two elements to this crisis that should be troubling to liberal democracies. The first revolves around the political and economic fallout associated with the disparity of scarcity. The availability of adequate water supplies and the knowledge to optimize the economic, social and environmental benefits which those supplies can bestow is now seen as a major defining element of the future viability of any given nation. As presently managed, the planet's supply of fresh water is insufficient to meet the human demands of many of the world's fastest-growing countries. In short, water is rapidly becoming a depleted global resource, and sovereign access to it is likely to become an explosive political trigger point in the realignment of nations and regions around the emerging realities associated with human existence on a hotter, and in many places drier, planet. As Steven Solomon puts it, water's historically discreet role in the building and sustaining of human civilizations is about to take centre stage. Put plainly, global political, economic and demographic power is about to realign around reliable, high-quality water supplies. From Calgary to Calcutta, struggles over such realignments are already happening.

The second element of this crisis relates to the increasingly serious problem we have created for ourselves by taking so much water away from nature for our own purposes. Unless we can quickly create new and more efficient ways to manage water, reallocating water back to nature will be difficult if not impossible in many places, which in itself will contribute to a vicious circle of further environmental decline.

Without new economic structures that take into account the environmental costs and other externalities related to current patterns of water use, any economic opportunities associated with improved water management will be eclipsed by political turmoil brought about by the disparity of scarcity and by the decline in biodiversity-based planetary life-support functions upon which our current economic models rely for their vitality and resilience. This suggests that addressing the global water crisis demands nothing less than the long-overdue restructuring of our economic models as well as wholesale reform of water governance, not just in Canada but around the world.

WHERE CANADA STANDS IN THIS CHANGING WORLD

Even though passionate advocates for First Nations equity, water conservation and aquatic ecosystem restoration can be found in every region of Canada, most Canadians still take water completely for granted. The reason for this is simple. We have created an elaborate system that allows the great majority of Canadians to think someone else will always take care of water on their behalf. Until now, someone else always has. The engineers have done a great job of making water reliably available, at least in cities, which is where most people live. But we see now that there is a downside to their approach. It is as though all of our intelligence and energy has been applied to ensuring that the public doesn't really need to play anything more than a token part in water conservation and stewardship. Water is what reliably comes out of the tap or the bottle. You may not like the fact, but a whole industry exists to make sure Canadians don't have to worry. To save money and improve convenience, we have unwittingly created an industry that for decades has advanced partial solutions that, over time and on our insistence, have created larger problems which we find difficult to address.

In the real world of everyday water management, it is widely recognized that it is going to be more expensive and more complicated to guarantee reliable supplies of high-quality water for our society in the future. It is also realized that the scale and capacity of our systems must increase. While innovations in technology will be helpful, sooner or later technological proxies will not be enough to address the problems we are creating for ourselves. It is only a matter of time before Canadians will have to face their own wastefulness. It won't be long before we will have to become as conscious of water conservation and water-quality protection as the rest of the world.

Understanding what is happening to our water cannot be confined to professional water-management circles. It also has to exist universally at the public level, where everyday people must be called upon to turn our current thinking – where we take as much as we want, end of story – on its head, and instead consider these questions: how much water must stay in natural systems, and how much of what remains may flow through the nation's industrial, agricultural and municipal taps? Water is something we all have to understand and take responsibility to participate in decisions about. Unless everyone participates in solutions to water supply and quality issues, we will be unable to reform our water ethic and will continue to run the risk of falling victim to our own habits.

FIRST, THERE ARE MYTHS WE NEED TO DISPEL

Before we can even begin to imagine a new water ethic for Canada there are a number of myths we must eliminate. The first is that we have limitless water abundance. If we do not dispel this myth, we will continue to make public-policy choices based on false assumptions which hurt many of us now and could have even more undesirable ecological, social and political consequences in the future.

We may have 20 per cent of the world's total fresh water, but we only have about 2850 cubic kilometres, or roughly 6.5 per cent, of the world's total *renewable* water – that is, the volume of water that gets refreshed annually by the hydrological cycle. This is the dividend we gain each year from our natural capital. Most of the water we have on the land in Canada – most of our natural capital – is water that was left on the landscape after the last ice age. We should also recognize that most of our water is in the north and flowing away from where we need it, away from where most Canadians live, namely within 300 kilometres of the US border.

The second myth we have to dispel is that we are world leaders in the management of water. We are good at engineering, yes, but we are not world leaders in the management of water. In fact, we are among the world's greatest water wasters and polluters. Great opportunity exists in changing that, in getting us closer to sustainability.

Another myth we have to get rid of is that proper management of water will make everyone happy. Very difficult trade-offs will mean that consensus will not be achievable on all water issues. This means that higher levels of government will have to assert leadership on important water matters on behalf of all Canadians, regardless of the location of their city, reserve or province. A good place for this leadership to begin is with a re-examination of what actually constitutes a right to water.

NEW ETHICAL MODELS FROM WHICH TO CHOOSE

As Carolyn Merchant points out in *Water Ethics*, there are a number of ethical frameworks from which humanity can choose at this critical point in our development.

Egocentric ethics focuses on the self. It seeks the maximization of individual self-interest based on the claim that what is good for the individual is good for society as a whole. This ethical framework derives principally from the ideas of Thomas Hobbes, John Locke and Adam Smith.

Anthropocentric ethics focuses on human society as a whole, seeking the greatest good for the greatest number of people over the longest period of time. It is an ethical framework derived principally from notions of utility developed by philosophers such as John Stuart Mill, Gifford Pinchot and Barry Commoner.

Ecocentric ethics focuses on the broader cosmos. It encourages the development of society based on awareness of our connections with and membership in the global ecological reality. This ethical framework derives from the ideas of 20th century ecologists such as Aldo Leopold, Rachel Carson and members of the Deep Ecology movement. These ideals are also reflected in Buddhism and many of the traditional moral, spiritual and ethical beliefs and practices of indigenous peoples worldwide.

Partnership ethics focuses on people and nature. This framework calls for equity between humans and between human and non-human communities; moral consideration for both humans and other species; respect for cultural diversity and biodiversity; and ecologically sound management that is consistent with the healthy perpetuation of both human and non-human life.

Partnership ethics emphasizes equity for all that exists today and in the future. It proposes that the greatest good for human and non-human communities resides in their mutual, living interdependence. This ethical framework derives largely from a growing community of ecologists and social scientists behind the emerging conservation biology movement, and there is increasing support for it, especially among upcoming generations, who in workshops across the country have already committed to talking in earnest about what the future would look like if such a framework were to be implemented. This ethic also is deeply understood by traditional indigenous peoples around the world.

RE-EVALUATING OUR CURRENT ETHIC

As previously noted, the partnership ethic stands in bold opposition to our current water ethic in Canada. Whether acknowledged or not, a principal element of the contemporary water ethic being practised in this country today is the primacy of human dominion over water. This ethic is founded upon the widely held belief that water should be viewed as a "natural resource," to be exploited at any time at humanity's sole discretion as with other "natural resources." Regardless of any other uses natural resources may need to be put to now or in the future, human uses and needs automatically take priority. This view has dominated our way of thinking in Canada for so long that our priority claims to water are codified through our oldest institutions, from property and related legal rights to social conventions and religious traditions.

The view that humans should have priority use of water, however, is now being widely challenged. The main criticism is that current notions of human priority are so self-centred, self-serving and patriarchal that they offer no room for women, non-Western peoples in general or other species to have standing in the moral community in which decisions about the allocation and use of water are made. But this is not the end of the criticism. Not even enlightened participatory and integrated management approaches are seen as having the power to overcome fragmented institutional structures, competing or conflicting government mandates, outdated water pricing policies (which often wrongfully attempt to price water itself rather than pricing the service), imbalanced sectoral water allocation priorities, continued reliance on expensive supply augmentation to address increasing demand, and the delegation of basin-level responsibilities without concomitant devolution of power and financial resources in decentralization plans. Together these problems are seen by critics of the human-priority ethic to be elements of a vicious circle in which the deteriorating status of water systems will ultimately result in deteriorating livelihoods and quality of life for many more Canadians.

But opposition to the current system goes even deeper than concerns about equity, institutional fragmentation and institutional territoriality. The main reason why the ethical argument that humans should have unquestioned priority claim to water is being rejected is that, on the evidence, it simply doesn't work at the most basic level of sustainability. It doesn't work because, as a consequence of its effect on biodiversity-based planetary life-support system functions, the human choice to place ourselves in dominion has been shown over time to undermine the ecological foundation of life on Earth. And it is this foundation that makes life not only possible but meaningful, not just in Canada but everywhere on the globe.

Examples of the failure of human dominion to contribute to sustainability are emerging in unexpected places. It has become widely held in Europe, for example, that if pollution and contamination of the waters of the Danube continue, the peoples of the 18 nations that share the river will destroy a source of their own livelihoods and compromise the quality of life of future generations for the sake of insignificant and short-lived economic and other perceived benefits. In so doing they may also undermine the life-giving and climate-stabilizing influences of natural ecosystem function. The moral and ethical implications of such short-sightedness are becoming increasingly difficult to ignore, as are the causes of our current failure to arrive at sustainability.

We have known for a long time that excluding nature from having rights was likely a bad idea, both practically and morally. As early as three centuries ago, even John Locke had reasoned that humanity should take from the ecological commons "only as there is enough and as good left for others." Peter Brown of Natural Resource Sciences and School of Environment at McGill University takes up Locke's argument in chapter 19 of *Water Ethics*, "Are There Any Natural Resources?"

Brown makes the case that the anthropocentric assumptions of contemporary resource economics are entirely inadequate, if not completely misplaced. Like many other observers, Brown disputes the validity of attempting to include nature in contemporary economic calculations by coming up with monetary values for "ecosystem services." Arguments offered in favour of this economic approach claim that when the monetary value of "nature" at last becomes high enough, then attention will be duly focused on protecting it.

Critics like Brown argue, however, that while this argument may appeal rhetorically, it presents a false picture of humanity's place in the world. Why, critics ask, should all of the millions of non-human species that make up this world be in service to us? When will the same ecosystems get to do similar evaluations of us? And when that happens, how will the rest of nature judge the fact that one species of the probably 15 million that exist on Earth permits itself to use, solely for its own purposes, 40 per cent of the total amount of photosynthesis that takes place on this planet each year?

Critics of market fundamentalism such as Brown further argue that economic anthropocentrism legitimizes and extends the morally indefensible mainstream view that it is possible and even somehow desirable to reduce all of the astoundingly diverse relationships that compose our world to self-referential market terms. They argue that the rights of other species to claim air, water, territory and necessities of life – indeed their right to merely exist – are legitimate and must be taken seriously in law and in the practice of water management. They must each have their voice, their rights in the system. Without this, we will not achieve sustainability.

Judging by what is happening elsewhere in the world, these are not arguments that can be easily dismissed. Our current way of living on the Canadian patch of Earth is not sustainable. The reason for this is that contemporary models of a competitive economy in our free-market system do not adequately approximate either economic or environmental reality. These models make irresponsible assumptions, such as the endless availability of unlimited inputs (which we term natural resources and cheap labour). They have the unrealistic – many say impossible – goal of continuous, limitless economic growth. While markets may balance supply and demand in the present, they cannot accurately capture the potential value of anything we consider important or desirable in the future. Current resource economics models discount the value of the negative effects of increasingly scarce water supplies and the deterioration of the quality of those supplies in the future. This leads to unrealistically low current prices for water use, which encourages excessively high rates of use in the present. While such valuations may be very helpful to private interests in the present, the risk is that current laws and practices will result in irreversible changes in the quantity and quality of water available in the future. Finally, these models persistently refuse to build into supply and demand the true costs of production: the "goods and services" that nature provides for free, such as pollution storage and absorption and the supply of material inputs.

Emerging ethical considerations also recognize that the needs of future generations may not be easy to meet, if only because we have already done so much damage to the world. Humanity today is actively engaged in the rapid, ongoing simplification of the planet's ecosystem composition and function. This is happening at a rate that is now demonstrably faster than photosynthesis or the natural selection capacity of DNA can compensate for. The fear is that the direct costs to our economy associated with ecosystem change and damage related to climate change will be so great that we will not be able to afford to protect ourselves and still maintain current levels of prosperity. There is a growing fear that adapting to such threats as climate change may in the end be far more expensive than mitigating those effects while it was still possible to do so.

It is now clear that the urgency of preserving the capacity for natural system self-organization and maintenance can no longer be ignored in economic models if we are to achieve sustainability in the future. This suggests that the ethics that drove water management decisions in the past have to be reconciled immediately with the emerging ethical demand that actions in the present not degrade future human and non-human life. A principled water ethic would argue that one generation should not be allowed to take unfair advantage of future generations through unjust exploitation of water that is available to them. Uses and negative economic externalities that do not sustain the capacity for natural system self-organization and maintenance and provide for intergenerational access to adequate water should therefore be limited or prohibited. The sooner this happens, the better our chance of achieving sustainability will be.

SITING A NEW CANADIAN WATER ETHIC

As Rajendra Pradhan and Ruth Meinzen-Dick point out in *Water Ethics*, three established interests are converging in the water management debate. Advocates of economic instruments generally align themselves with privatization, while supporters of the human-rights value of water usually support community management. A third emerging interest, which places the highest value on environmental uses of water, argues that human uses should be minimized in order to protect natural habitats. At the moment – as Pradhan and Meinzen-Dick demonstrate – this three-way debate appears to be generating more heat than light. The management of water in this complicated period of human history cannot be defined by three competing ethics, if only because First Nations values – which place humans as a co-partner with the rest of the animate and inanimate inhabitants of the Earth – are given no place in the debate. In order to assure the broadest base of support for a new water ethic for Canada, that ethic has to incorporate the most effective elements of each of these value systems and must do so in a manner that employs effective economic, legal and ethical incentives to ensure equity of supply and quality to everyone in society as well as to nature.

With the rapid emergence of the discipline of ecohydrology, it is increasingly recognized that the strictly utilitarian approaches we have employed to supply water to humanity in past centuries no longer work and will fail as populations continue to grow and as our global climate changes. The new ethic we need to create should advance our society toward a historic shift in the way we regard water as it relates to our way of life. What is needed is an integrated, holistic approach to water that views people and water as interconnected parts of a greater ecological and existential whole that includes natural, agricultural, urban, industrial and aesthetic elements. What is needed is a new way of co-existing with water that achieves the objectives of the partnership ethic.

In this new ethic it would be seen that nature cannot just be the place where we send water if there is enough left after we have taken what we want. This new ethic would recognize that in order to provide valuable, life-giving ecological services to people, nature needs water too. Instead of continually investing in how we can further manipulate and control rivers, streams, lakes and aquifers to meet ever-expanding human water demands, we should be investing instead in ways of accommodating the ecological requirements of freshwater ecosystems so that those ecosystems can continue to prime the hydrologic pump and maintain the planetary life-support system function and regulation we and the rest of nature depend on. There is no question that an ethic of this kind is necessary to make the protection of freshwater ecosystems central to human presence on this planet. Though this may appear highly idealistic, it is no more radical a proposal than suggesting that a building be given a solid foundation before adding 50 storeys of apartments on top of it.

While everyone involved in water may be clear on which management tradition they belong to, not everyone can articulate their underlying water ethic or the ethics their respective efforts serve. Many sense that the things we are doing now are not working and will not work in the world we are creating. But when we contemplate change, we discover that the institutions we have created to govern the management of water, and the precedents those institutions have set, have hardened into the cement of sectoral habit and protective self-interest. To prevent being paralyzed by our past into inaction at a crucial turning point in the history of our country and of the planet, we need a new set of principles relating to how we wish to manage our country's water within the broader context of our vision for the future. In short, Canada needs a new water ethic. What might that look like?

PART THREE

Proposed Elements of a New Canadian Water Ethic

In examining the current, outdated state of water management in Canada, it becomes apparent that reform can be orchestrated around at least seven basic ethical principles. Each of these principles will need to be supported by changes in attitudes and practices in very specific areas.

PRINCIPLE 1
RECOGNIZE NATURE'S NEED FOR WATER

A viewpoint popularized by Herbert Hoover during the construction of the Grand Coulee Dam in Washington State in 1935 became the motto for an age of dam building in North

America that resulted in the alteration of flows in thousands of rivers, the displacement of millions of people and untold ecological damage worldwide. The motto was to the effect that every drop of water that ran to the sea without yielding its full commercial return to the nation was an economic waste.

The notion that a drop of water that flows past you unused is wasted has been completely dispelled in every region of the globe. We now realize that every drop of water in any given river system is fully utilized, whether by people, by agriculture or industry, by nature or in natural geophysical processes. If you don't believe this, you are invited to visit areas in British Columbia where saltwater incursion is destroying coastal aquifers, where estuaries are being ruined because river flows are so diminished by upstream use that they can no longer hold back the seawater.

There are cases on the west coast where communities that rely on the salmon fishery have to pump cold water from lakes into rivers to ensure there is enough water for salmon to swim and that the river water is cold enough that salmon can still spawn there. Even when we have a lot of water, we no longer have enough when and where we want to use it. Thus we find that, even in the midst of abundance, there is growing scarcity.

It is clear now that under the aegis of the "every drop we don't use is wasted" motto, we began dismantling a natural system that took billions of years to evolve, while ignorantly maintaining that ours were the only interests that mattered. We now know that engineering-based models of hydrological cycles did not take into account the actual behaviour of complex ecological systems and failed to predict catastrophic changes to biophysical processes caused by human interference in natural cycles brought about by large dams, extensive irrigation projects and the attendant changes in land cover. Though it is difficult to comprehend, the world's 45,000 large dams have changed the operation of the global water cycle.

Looking back on what historians have labelled a passing era of hydro-structuralism, many observers have argued that perhaps we should not have declared water a natural resource and should now retreat from that notion. Their argument is that we have to get water out of the human-centred policy universe. The first step in this process, they propose, is the recognition that engineering-based assertions of passive ecological stationarity are incorrect interpretations of the world and, as such, must cease now to be a foundation of Canada's water ethic.

We will not survive as a civilization unless the rights of people are balanced with the rights of nature. This suggests that we may need to consider water as something inherently unique and irreplaceable, as something that has legal status or at least the right to exist in the quality and quantity necessary to sustain natural functions upon which we also depend. Water ethicists would go further. Many maintain that a partnership ethic is required, one that holds that notions of the greatest good for the greatest number extend membership outward beyond our own species. As Carolyn Merchant has famously argued, sooner or later fish have to be at, not just on, the table.

Respected Canadian water-policy scholars such as the University of Waterloo's Rob de

Loë have pointed out that if we include nature's need for water, even Canada's abundant supplies are already fully allocated, either to persons or to members of the non-human community. Not even in Canada is there any excess water. While many Canadians still erroneously believe we have more water than we will ever need, this notion can only make sense from a completely human-centred point of view. All the fresh water in Canada – and all the fresh water everywhere else on the planet as well – is already used if not fully utilized in support of natural communities.

It follows, then, as Sandra Postel argues in "The Missing Piece: A Water Ethic," chapter 20 of *Water Ethics*, that an ethically based water policy must begin with the premise that all people and all living things have equal rights to enough water to assure their survival before some get more than enough. The extension of rights to rivers, aquatic plants, fish and the ecosystems they are all part of will not be easy to accomplish, but equity will only be achieved if all human and non-human players are at the table when the hand that is our collective future is dealt. Granting rights to ecosystems may mean we will have to pay agricultural producers and landowners to protect or provide important ecological and ecohydrological services that we cannot afford or do not know how to provide through technology. Considerable opportunity could exist in the future for those who understand and can act upon new ecoagricultural urgencies.

If we agree that a new Canadian water ethic must recognize that rivers in themselves and all the life forms that inhabit them have a right to water, then we may have to accept that there will be circumstances in which the water needs of aquatic ecosystems will have higher priority than those of irrigation or other uses. Some argue that this will prove as difficult a battle as the historic struggles for freedom for slaves and equal rights for women and indigenous peoples. History shows that those who possess rights tend to want to monopolize them.

To advance a water ethic that includes rights of rivers and ecosystems to their own water, we will need a thorough reassessment of the role ecosystems play in water supply and quality in the Canadian context. Minimal water supply to protect aquatic ecosystem integrity by itself is an inadequate measure of how much water we may need to share with nature. Because of the complexity of aquatic ecosystems and our very limited knowledge of larger, planetary-scale ecosystem connectivity and function, we may never know where such thresholds are until we have already crossed them. This suggests that what we really need to do is identify and agree on the optimal and necessary water requirements of each of these ecosystems in order to secure sustainable services to them and to people. Though much more needs to be done to ensure we actually adhere to the precautionary principles related to in-stream flows, some advances in the right direction have already been made in these domains.

Subprinciple 1
Meet Ecosystem Flow Needs

While we have somehow managed to build more than 600 major dams in Canada and divert more water than almost any other country, we do not appear to be able to come to agreement anywhere in the nation on necessary ecosystem flows to protect aquatic ecosystem health. This is likely due in great measure to our underlying lack of agreement as to what is worth "protecting" and to what extent. This, more than anything else, demonstrates the anthropogenic and utilitarian biases that currently dominate water management in Canada. The fact remains, however, that these biases are fundamentally contrary to a partnership approach with nature.

Traditionally, sovereign states have chosen to maintain ecosystem flow by mandating minimum water levels by administrative and often arbitrary fiat, by reserving water from appropriation, by putting conditions on water licences, by directing state agencies to acquire and hold ecosystem flow rights or by using the public-trust doctrine to establish that private rights do not supersede the state's responsibility to maintain aquatic ecosystem vitality.

While current rights structures have not adequately allowed for ecosystem flows, the growing realization of nature's need for water and the advent of better technologies for monitoring water use are putting growing pressure on established rights. In "Priming the Invisible Pump," chapter 9 in *Water Ethics*, authors Terry Anderson and Donald Leal cite the perspectives of US water law professor James Huffman, who has argued that sophisticated 21st-century flow-monitoring technologies can serve in-stream flow rights just as effectively as the barbed-wire technology of the 19th century served to define grazing-land property rights. Huffman goes on to assert that defining the parameters of eco-system flow rights are fundamentally no more difficult than defining the parameters of a right to divert water for agriculture or industry. The problem today is that current water allocations to agriculture and industry are tied to whole rafts of subsidies and other long-standing prec-edents that those sectors do not want the public or anyone else to interfere with or even know about. To open up for review and discussion the matter of water allocations for agriculture, for example, would inevitably lead to public pres-sure for badly needed, sweeping reform of the entire sector.

Thus we see that if you pull on the loose thread of water, the entire fabric of contemporary society feels it. Those most affected will react in any way necessary to prevent even the beginning of any unravelling. Politicians who know the most about these matters are invariably the ones from constituencies in which agriculture or industry interests have significant political power. In such situations, pulling too hard on the loose thread of water allocations would be political suicide.

Just because agriculture is a big economic driver, however, does not mean it should be declared off-limits to reform. Severe pollution of agricultural origin suggests an important federal role in water policy reform. As politically difficult as such a decision may be, sooner or later government simply has to acknowledge and enforce society's compliance with broader ethical rules (then made mandatory in law) to ensure that aquatic ecosystem needs are met. Failure to do so is tantamount to politically pronouncing that sustainability is beyond our collective grasp and that we must accept the decline of natural and agroecological systems as our fate as a society. Each delay in recognizing nature's need for water will make in-stream flow rights that much harder to establish in the future. International example suggests it would be wise to establish these rights while discussing thorny issues around limiting growth in population and water demand before exacerbation of those issues makes it almost impossible to do so.

Subprinciple 2
Appreciate the Difference between "Blue" Water versus "Green" Water

The growing realization of nature's need for water revolves around new understanding about how different kinds of ecosystems generate, capture, purify and release water. It also revolves around new ideas about its function, including the separation of "blue" water from "green." Blue water is the water that appears on the surface of the Earth as streams, rivers and lakes. Green water is precipitation that naturally infiltrates the ground to become soil moisture. Green water evaporates as it is drawn up by plants, to become available again to form precipitation. It has been estimated that two-thirds of all precipitation over continental land masses can be defined as green water. Natural vegetation, forests and food crops all evapotranspire green water back into the atmosphere, but at different rates. From this we understand how human-caused land-use impacts alter not only how much water is available as soil moisture but also how much will be released again by vegetation to be available in the form of precipitation locally and elsewhere. We also learn that land use can be proactively managed to enhance the hydrological cycle.

Research into the influence of green water on ecosystem function has demonstrated that a whole series of interactions contribute to what is now being called "ecohydrosolidarity." Ecohydrosolidarity can be defined as the combined result of water's dominating but interactive influence on terrestrial and aquatic ecosystem function in a given landscape. If we accept that intergenerational equity requires sustainable land productivity and long-term ecological resilience in order to maintain and enhance the contributions landscape makes to human well-being, then water's role in this process becomes of great interest to us.

Water plays a fundamental role in maintaining the ecosystem's resilience. When human activities reduce ecological function through land-use impacts, water's actual and potential role in the self-organizing processes of living systems is diminished. If this role is reduced below certain thresholds, affected systems can no longer act as buffers to disturbance. We now know that water supply to nature is crucial in preventing ecosystems from passing from one state to another, such as prairies becoming deserts or forests turning into grasslands. The careful capture of as much water as possible in upstream areas by rainwater harvesting and through ecological capture has also been proven to assist in maintaining resilience that prevents or moderates the possible effects of both flooding and drought while at the same time generating greater flow volume downstream. In other words, providing water for productive natural ecosystem function in the end ensures there is more water available generally and therefore more that is reliably available for human purposes. Thus we find that the careful management of water's role in ecosystem function is a form of insurance against threats to the stability of the life systems upon which humans depend for their livelihood and prosperity. But to be of any use, we have to buy that insurance.

Science has identified the kinds of impacts that cause the loss of resilience in natural systems that in turn results in a cascade of effects leading toward irreversible ecological change. These impacts include downstream lake and river eutrophication; agricultural impacts on soil moisture as a result of grazing and reductions in vegetation cover; the replacement of deep-rooted trees and grasses with annual crops; and changes in climate as a result of the cumulative effects of catastrophic ecological regime changes. All of these impacts have made their appearance in Canada recently. Each of these trends predicts that the central prairie region, for example, is becoming increasingly vulnerable to exactly the kinds of regime shifts that only a different, more integrated way of managing land and water can prevent. As our climate warms we should expect similar effects in other bioregions.

Ecohydrological research has demonstrated that careful management of ecological composition can actually increase or decrease the amount of water a given ecosystem generates, both green water and the precipitation that green water can help generate. In experiments in the arid Middle East, for example, ecohydrological approaches to the integrated management of natural, agricultural and urban ecosystems have generated an increase of as much as 40 per cent in the total amount of water locally within the system. From this we see that such integration will not only reduce our vulnerability but also generate substantial agricultural productivity and quality of life benefits while at the same time advancing sustainability goals. If should be noted, however, that the net benefits of such gains may be lost if increases in population result in loss of ecological integrity elsewhere.

The sustainability challenge of the 21st century will be fivefold. It will demand that we learn how to make the most productive use of rainfall; optimize the role of fresh water in the self-organizing processes of living systems; learn how to generate the most water and the most services possible from such systems; put that water and those services to the most productive use, not just for people but for the broader life community; and ensure that the net sustainability gains generated by such activities are not lost to uncontrolled growth or contradictory economic development.

Hope for the future resides in the possibility of a radically new water management ethic emerging from the application of ecohydrological principles that are at the heart of new ways of valuing water.

Subprinciple 3
Practise the Precautionary Principle

Many of the decisions we must make will be difficult. History has shown us that when citizens insist on doing what is right, the push-back from governments and business can sometimes be severe. In 1991, for example, when the town of Hudson, Quebec, wished to protect its people, lands and waters from the hazards of lawn chemicals by implementing a local ban on the sale and cosmetic use of those chemicals, it was sued by the manufacturers whose products were banned. After a long legal battle, Hudson was successful when the Supreme Court of Canada upheld the town's right to, among other things, rely on the precautionary principle as a valid and legally acceptable basis upon which to make their sound decision.[1] The example set by Hudson spurred many other municipalities and provinces in Canada to enact similar bans of pesticides. It took courageous leadership, however, to effect this change. Such leadership, as we will see, must be one of the pillars of a new Canadian water ethic.

The federal government long ago accepted the precautionary principle as valid, and vowed to rely on it when making decisions, yet the principle has failed to systematically influence water-related decisions at any level. In fact, it is probably trite to say that the opposite has occurred in Canada. The precautionary principle is, regrettably, a noble-sounding and seldom used tool, because it would require making dramatically different decisions.

This failure of governments to act in a way that safeguards Canadians and the environment from exposure to toxic chemicals must stop if we are to achieve any meaningful level of environmental or economic sustainability in this country. If we are engaged in a relationship that is critical to the future of life on Earth – the relationship we have with water – and we are uncertain as to the environmental soundness of a proposed decision, the precautionary principle would provide us the answer to this question: *why risk it?* To create a sustainable future, we will have to collectively and consistently answer that we refuse to take unreasonable risks with the protection of our water or our environment.

Subprinciple 4
Emerging Ecohydrological Perspectives Will Drive a Different Future

Conservation in the future will likely be couched in broader ecohydrological terms. The day may be coming when sustainability will force us to integrate natural, agricultural and urban ecosystem function into a unified whole. Total ecosystem function will be managed so as to preserve the greatest possible amount of natural water for human and ecosystem use while at the same time protecting or restoring ecosystem services we can't afford to or don't know how to provide otherwise. Wetland restoration is an example of a matter where total ecosystem function must be considered. According to a number of estimates, Canada has lost perhaps as much as 70 per cent of its wetlands, which means we have lost a great deal of our country's natural ecological resilience. We know now that despite monumental efforts by Ducks Unlimited and others to restore wetlands on the prairies, restoration is not keeping up with destruction. Moreover, restored wetlands seldom provide more than half the ecological services such ecosystems provided in their natural state. This has important implications in the larger context of nature's need for water. What it means is that if we are unable to restore wetlands to the Canadian prairies, then that loss has to be made up elsewhere or we and the world will continue to suffer broader declines in planetary life-support function.

This suggests once again that the time may also be coming when citizens will have to pay for ecosystem services. When that happens, urbanites will pay others such as farmers to generate those services, which will be seen to have a value, at least in terms of willingness to pay, that is equal to or greater than the value of many contemporary crops. As pointed out earlier, there will ultimately be huge opportunity in this for those who know how to profit from broader agroecological thinking.

PRINCIPLE 2
WATER IS INEXTRICABLY LINKED TO HUMAN HEALTH

A wellspring is a place where a spring or series of springs breaks out of the ground. Wellsprings are often the origins or sources of streams and rivers. More broadly, the word "wellspring" is used to describe an abundant source or beginning. In terms of Canadian identity, water is the wellspring of who we are as a people. Though we are often so close to it that we don't see it, our relationship to water is what makes us unique and healthy as a people.

There is a reason a well is called a well. Clean, reliably available water is the foundation of human wellness. It is also the basis of all ecological function – the planetary, biodiversity-based life-support system function upon which all living things depend. When we talk about the decline of water quality globally or locally, we are not just talking about an environmental concern. We are talking about an impending existential crisis, one that affects not only our surroundings but our very being. The state of our waters is inextricably linked to how we feel about ourselves and how healthy we are as people.

Subprinciple 1
Establish and Enforce Mandatory, Legally Binding Drinking Water Standards

> *We are the only developed country in the world without enforceable water quality standards.*
> — DR. KAREN BAKKER

Though responsibility for water quality and management is primarily a provincial jurisdiction, both federal and provincial governments are responsible for working together under the terms of the Guidelines for Canadian Drinking Water Quality, published by Health Canada since 1968. The responsibility for the creation and updating of these guidelines falls to the

Federal–Provincial–Territorial Committee on Drinking Water, made up of representatives from Health Canada, Environment Canada and each province and territory. These guidelines are meant to comprise a set of standards aimed at assuring that provincial, territorial, municipal and private water users and suppliers are able to protect human health over a lifetime of consumption. The guidelines are meant to apply to both public water distribution and private water supply where individuals rely on groundwater and wells for drinking and other uses.

It is important to note, however, that these guidelines are not legally binding. Provincial or territorial adherence to them is purely voluntary. The standards are no more than they describe themselves to be: just guidelines. Individual provinces and territories are invited to use these federal guidelines as a basis for their own enforceable standards or regulations. Or they may simply use them as guidelines, as some provinces do. Even on First Nation reserves, where the federal government has jurisdiction, the guidelines are not applied as mandatory. Mandatory, legally binding national drinking water standards should be one of the principles of the new Canadian water ethic.

Subprinciple 2
Recognize the Hazards and
Costs of Polluting Water

All living things require water of adequate quality to survive. Despite this, we fail to recognize that many of our decisions are directly threatening the future of ecosystems and species, including humans, worldwide. It is well documented that amounts of toxic chemicals in all environments on Earth are increasing and that they are persistent once present. Unlike the pollution of the past, which was visible in the smokestacks and dying rivers that so characterized the beginning of the industrial age, pollution now is invisible, non-point-source, widespread and long-term. We have a hard time seeing and feeling – in the immediate way that smokestacks allow us to see – the changes that result from exposure to this kind of pollution. But despite the lack of awareness of many Canadians, genetic and other changes are occurring with greater frequency in many species, including humans, as a result of un-known or difficult to pinpoint exposures, some at extremely low levels previously thought to be safe. While many of us have trusted our governments to protect us, our children and nature from unnecessary exposure, it appears that this is not occurring as it should and as it must if we are to sustain ourselves as a society.

A growing body of research is generating concern about the lack of consumer protection and government safeguards against many toxic chemicals, including those that end up in our waterways from sources such as personal-care products, electronics, toys and other consumer goods. By the time we are exposed to these chemicals, either directly or through ingesting food or water that contains them, many other species have already been exposed. The endocrine-disrupting ability of many of these chemicals threatens the sustainability of ecosystems and the species within them, including us.

Endocrine disruptors are substances that mimic or interfere with the function of hormones in the body. They may turn on, shut off or modify signals that hormones carry and thus affect the normal functioning of tissues and organs. Endocrine signals govern virtually every organ and process in the body. This means that when outside chemicals interfere with those systems, the effects show up as many different diseases and conditions, some of which we are only just learning to recognize as being the result of endocrine disruption.

Over the past 20 years, concerns have been raised about observed increases in endocrine-sensitive health outcomes. According to the National Institute of Environmental Health Sciences in the United States, breast and prostate cancer are on the rise;[2] there was a fourfold increase in ectopic pregnancies in the US between 1970 and 1987;[3] and there has been an approximately 50 per cent decrease in sperm count worldwide over the second half of the 20th century.[4] This decrease in human reproductive capacity has been attributed in large measure to the introduction into the environment of exactly the kinds of substances many advocates don't mention in defending the environmental performance of oil sands operators.

Researchers are finding that the effects

of exposure to endocrine disruptors can be observed long after the actual exposure has ceased, and that some of these substances can cause cancer in humans. Unfortunately, such substances have a bad habit of ending up in unexpected places – places very close to home, at least for some.

Economists around the world are now warning of an emerging new scarcity that will affect every sector of our economy. This growing scarcity is defined by very real limits that are becoming all too apparent in the capacity of the environment to absorb and neutralize the unprecedented streams of waste that humanity releases into it. With less and less capacity to absorb such wastes, the costs of getting rid of them are continuing to rise.

The gravity of this problem may not be apparent until we realize that we ourselves are becoming walking waste dumps. A recent study by Environmental Defence tested Canadians for the presence of 88 harmful chemicals in their bodies. A First Nations volunteer from a remote community on Hudson Bay was found to have 51 of the chemicals. Blood and urine samples from a Toronto mother were found to contain 38 re-productive and respiratory toxins, 19 chemicals that disrupt hormones, and 27 carcinogens. One of the co-authors of this book was part of this study. She discovered that she carried around in her body some 26 carcinogens, 15 hormonal disruptors, 14 respiratory toxins and 35 repro-ductive and developmental toxicants.

There are now communities around the Great Lakes where mercury levels have risen so high that a neurological disease similar to the one discovered in Minamata, Japan, in the 1950s has begun to appear in Canadian children. It is very difficult to keep harmful chemicals out of our water and out of our bodies, especially when they are everywhere in the environment. Unless we do something about it, Canadians appear doomed to spend our entire lives saturated like French fries with hydrocarbon residues.

We did not consent to being exposed to these chemicals. Moreover, we have limited knowledge of their long-term effects. There are, however, some well-known and documented cases where the harmful effects of such expo-sure have been clearly identified. Bisphenol A, for example, has been banned from plastics. But too little is being done too late. In northern Canada the government has warned that Inuit women are so contaminated with harmful substances that they should not feed their babies breast milk. Imagine being so contaminated that you cannot feed your own child. What kind of society would tolerate such a thing?

In allowing the proliferation of chemicals in our environment and our bodies, governments have not fulfilled the fiduciary relationship they have with us to act in the best interests of Canadians and our environment. To prevent harm. To apply the precautionary principle. A new water ethic requires Canadians to insist on prevention in cases involving environmental chemicals. Such chemicals must not be allowed into the Canadian marketplace or released into our water until they are proven safe, not just as individual substances but in terms of their collective cumulative impact. Only this approach will protect the long-term health of the environment and all species that depend on it. This must be a fundamental tenet of a new water ethic.

Subprinciple 3
The Right to Clean Water Must
Extend to Everyone

At the time of this writing, the only provincial or territorial jurisdiction in Canada that legally grants its citizens the right to clean water is the Northwest Territories. The federal government has backed away from active implementation of its water responsibilities in many areas, not the least of which is the protection of First Nation waters and the provision of safe drinking water to First Nations. It is only a matter of time before our failure to adequately and consistently address long-standing human rights issues alters existing water allocation and use rights in parts of Canada. Many treaties include clauses related to First Nations rights to water quality as well as quantity. Despite billions spent on water security on reserves, the problem is not going away. People on First Nations reserves are still 90 times more likely than the rest of us to be without piped water. Water security conditions on many Canadian reserves are no better than those that exist in the developing world. Some would argue

that we cannot say we have any ethics at all related to water until this issue is resolved.

PRINCIPLE 3
HONOUR THE FIRST NATIONS WATER ETHIC

*Post-colonial consciousness of indigenous peoples
contains desires to create a new world based upon a
fusion of Western and Aboriginal ideas.*
— DR. DAVID NEWHOUSE,
ONONDAGA NATION

Albert Marshall is a Mi'gmaq Elder of the Eska-
soni First Nation in Mi'gma'gi. The territory of
his people is also known as Nova Scotia, and in
describing these lands in this way, highlighting
the overlapping layers of use, entitlement and
connection, we are practising what Marshall
has called "two-eyed seeing." With one eye, we
can see the strengths of indigenous peoples'
knowledge systems and values, and with the
other we can choose to see the strengths of
Western ways of knowing. When we recognize
the worldviews, history and principles of multiple nations – indigenous and non-indigenous –
we are practising two-eyed seeing. With the aid

of two-eyed seeing, we also can choose to learn from one another, to engage in co-learning: creating, building upon, using, modifying new systems of understanding, awareness and thought that can create a better world for both humans and nature. A decolonized world. A respectful set of relationships between indigenous peoples and non-indigenous peoples, and between all of us and everything else that also needs and wants functioning ecosystems.

Two-eyed seeing leads us to a new water ethic that is based on two truths: the sacred connection between our bodies and the world, and the need for reconciliation. By *truth*, we mean we must recognize and redress the effects of past and current activities (and the decisions or lack thereof that have enabled those activities) on rivers, streams, wetlands, lakes and oceans. By *reconciliation*, we mean there must be a change in behaviour regarding our use of water that recognizes both the instrumental and the intrinsic values of water and, through this recognition, creates a new future for all inhabitants of Canada. Truth and reconciliation, we should all agree, are necessary in order for all Canadians to be able to fulfill both our common and our particular responsibilities to water.

Human decisions and actions would be different if our goals were always focused on restoring, preserving and preventing harm to the sacred connection with water that we and all other entities that make up this earth have. Our actions would be different if we felt the emotional pain of bad water decisions just as acutely as if water were a member of the family. Such an ethic would also mean that all other beings of the world (whether animate or inanimate and regardless of what you put into which category or whether you create categories at all) would be privy to that same level of restoration, preservation and prevention.

Numerous First Nations have been asserting their water rights, and they are increasingly turning to the courts for assistance. Recent legal settlements over treaty-related water issues demonstrate that the rights of First Nations to pursue the water ethic they founded in Canada have not been extinguished. This suggests that the rights of non-indigenous Canadians to a water ethic different from the one that has emerged in the last century have not been extinguished either, as we are partners to and beneficiaries of the treaties with indigenous peoples that built this country. In order that all Canadians do not lose the rights they agreed to through those treaties, however, a new water ethic has to be articulated and the rights to practise it have to be asserted. A new water ethic based on ecohydrological principles is consistent with a water ethic many First Nations wish to perpetuate, through implementation of Aboriginal title, inherent rights, treaties, land claims settlements and self-government agreements. This also suggests that if Canadians want a new water ethic – indeed a water democracy – now may be a good time to create one.

The Northwest Territories Water Ethic

The recently ratified Northwest Territories Water Strategy illustrates how First Nations water ethics can be effectively put into practice at the watershed level. Passed by the legislature of the Northwest Territories in the spring of 2010, the Northern Voices, Northern Waters strategy is unique in four ways. First, it was developed in full collaboration with the indigenous governments who will be affected by it and upon whom responsibility for its implementation will ultimately fall. Second, the strategy was developed before the region faced a crisis of either water availability or quality. This will allow those responsible for implementing the strategy to stay ahead of emerging problems. Third, the strategy commits to placing nature's need for water first in governmental decision-making. Finally, the Northern Voices, Northern Waters strategy is unique in that it is founded upon ecohydrological principles supported by both traditional knowledge and western science that in tandem support local cultural values and relationship to place. It appears to be a strategy based upon the ideas of two-eyed seeing.

The strategy recognizes that the Mackenzie Basin may be one of the linchpins holding North America's water–ice–climate equilibrium together. If the stability of this important ecohydrologic system is compromised, it could cause the Earth's climate to wobble out of its current equilibrium, with implications for all the ecosystems on the continent whose stability is coupled to current climate variability. The strategy also recognizes, however, that it is possible for people to live – and develop economically – within the constraints of a water ethic that recognizes the water needs of people and nature.

In the Mackenzie Basin, Canada has the opportunity to get it right, to plan ahead in order to avoid bitter tensions later over the need for expensive restoration or compensation for lost ecosystem function. Getting it right will require that federal, provincial, territorial and Aboriginal governments come together at the scale that matters most for water – the entire watershed – to transcend political boundaries and develop a plan that protects these remarkable rivers and respects the established rights of the peoples who depend on the Mackenzie for their livelihood and their cultural identity.

PRINCIPLE 4
WE MUST MAKE A STRONG PUBLIC COMMITMENT TO EXPAND SAFE, RELIABLE PUBLIC DRINKING WATER SUPPLY

Subprinciple 1
At a Basic Level, Water Is a Human Right

The goal in Canada should be to ensure that

everyone in the country has a safe, reliable, public drinking water supply. Like healthcare, such supply should be part of the social contract we have with our governments. Sufficient supplies of free or low-cost water must be guaranteed for basic individual human needs and to meet nature's needs. A new water ethic in Canada would demand this as one of the conditions government must fulfill on behalf of those it governs, in exchange for the latter's acceptance of being governed.

Subprinciple 2
Beyond the Level of Individual Need,
the Use of Water Is a Privilege, not a Right

While it will be important to explore variable pricing instruments to encourage water conservation, the pricing of the delivery of water must be structured in such a way that it acknowledges a fundamental human right to enough water for individual needs and does not discriminate in any way against the poor.

That said, governments should not be permitted to lose control of pricing nor to lose control of or give away the right to use water on a permanent basis. Since the use of water over and above personal needs is to be considered a privilege and not a right, pricing that is specifically related to the cost of this privilege must be clearly identified as being completely exclusive of the cost of the water itself. To achieve the goals of a new Canadian water ethic, water must remain a common good subject to the principles of public trust and fiduciary. And while some aspects of the treatment and delivery of water may under certain circumstance be granted to others, the use, control and protection of water must be held firmly in the control of government, for which the government must be fully, immediately and transparently accountable.

The management and protection of water in Canada must be seen as a centuries-long project on which the foundation of our society depends for its stability and sustainability. Water has to be managed for the long term, not just for the term of office of a given party or leader or during the heyday of a single industry or economic activity. This means we cannot tolerate sectors or interests that try to bully a government or the public into believing that the privilege of using water should be granted to them as a right just because of their economic influence at a given moment in history. Neither can we continue to tolerate the special pleading so damaging to our water resources that is so much a part of contemporary political lobbying.

No government should be allowed to lose control of water within its jurisdiction as a result of lack of regulation of permits granted for the privilege of using water. We should not allow markets or exchanges in which financial investments could be made that would make it unduly difficult or impossible to restore water use to the public trust. Similarly, we should not permit alienation of the privilege of using water to such an extent that the public no longer has effective control over its use. Neither should water rights ever be granted on such terms as to suggest that the privilege of using water for any given purpose is permanent and unfettered by government control. There are limits to the extent to which access to water can be both a human right and an economic good. Given the uncertainties of future water supply and quality, we should never allow private interests to use the considerable political means at their disposal to transform a contingent water use privilege into a permanent property right.

Subprinciple 3
Bottled Water Is Not a Solution

In many political and most corporate circles in Canada, it is widely held that the marketplace will take care of the country's growing water woes. There is no evidence, however, that this is happening – or will happen – to the extent required for achieving sustainability. Nor is there any evidence from international example that suggests market instruments alone address water supply or quality issues in any enduring way. Without government control and oversight, markets tend to take care of themselves first and do not always solve the problems they were directed through public policy to address.

The classic example of how market-based solutions drive us to do everything available to us except actually address the problem is bottled water. There are places in the world where bottled water is necessary and, because of local water quality, likely always will be. In the developed world, however, the marketplace success of bottled water is a triumph of marketing over common sense and appropriate action.

We have allowed ourselves to be convinced through subtle and not so subtle manipulation of our desires to pay thousands of times more for what we already get almost for free. The irony is that we drink bottled water even though billions are being spent to ensure that the quality of our public drinking water is the best in the world. Meanwhile, a billion people on earth cannot afford reliable public water supplies or bottled water, and we say we can't afford to help them. If the $100-billion a year we spend on bottled water were committed instead to addressing the global water supply and sanitation crisis, there would be little need for bottled water in most parts of the world within a decade.

In *Bottled & Sold*, his landmark work on the story behind our obsession with bottled water, Peter Gleick argues that the world is in the midst of a major transition which he fears could be marked by the abandonment of our efforts to provide public drinking water for all, in favour of private-sector solutions.

Subprinciple 4
Recognize the Real Cost of Water Infrastructure

Inadequate infrastructure is one of the most serious challenges facing our water systems. Across Canada, many municipalities and First Nations are facing severe infrastructure deficits for both water and wastewater services. The federal government recently reported that the nation's wastewater treatment facilities had exhausted 63 per cent of their useful life by 2003. An Ontario report found that in that province alone, $30-billion to $40-billion of new investment in water and wastewater facilities was required. In Alberta, at least $290-million was required immediately in 2006, with perhaps a billion more in the coming decades.

In 2010 the Canadian Water Network estimated Canada's infrastructure maintenance deficit at $88.4-billion. At this time at least, that money does not exist, suggesting that many Canadian communities are going to face greater vulnerability to failure of their water treatment systems in the near future. As the Walkerton Inquiry warned, what happened in that small, pleasant Ontario town could happen almost anywhere in Canada.

In coming to terms with Canada's current drinking water challenges, it is important to understand that it costs a great deal of money to design, build and operate reliable water treatment systems. Historically, Canadians in general have not paid the true costs associated with drinking water supply. As of 2006, only 56 per cent of urban water in Canada was metered. As a result of the failure to meter use, Canadians are not forced to consider how much they use and are not generally motivated to practise conservation.

Since revenues collected from water users seldom reflect the true cost of supplying the water, municipalities do not always have the money they need to operate and maintain water treatment facilities to the necessary standard. This becomes an issue of asset management. As most revenues from municipal water supply go into general revenue accounts not linked in any way to replacement costs of such facilities, many Canadian communities do not have the capacity to cost-effectively manage the full life cycle of water treatment infrastructure in a way that will allow such facilities to pay for their own operation and for their ultimate replacement when they have reached the end of their useful life expectancy. As for First Nations, most have permanent shortfalls.

Municipalities rely upon federal and provincial grants to upgrade and replace facilities when they are no longer efficient or are too small to meet expanded needs created by population growth and economic development. The problem, however, is that much of Canada's water treatment and delivery infrastructure is almost the same age and will need replacing at about the same time. What we have done is little different than buying exactly the automobile you want – even if it was very expensive – and then not putting any money aside to properly maintain it or replace it when it wears out. Failing to price water high enough to maintain water infrastructure is a mistake that many countries around the world regret, and one we can avoid making in Canada.

We are not talking here about turning water into a commodity. We are talking about making sure our existing water infrastructure doesn't decline because our institutional arrangements related to its maintenance and replacement fail to work as promised, as they have done in so many places in the world. When water is free, or as close to free as governments can make it, no one thinks water has value, which in turn amplifies wasteful use. When public water utilities cannot recoup the cost of operation, maintenance and replacement of their water supply systems, they are forced to rely on government subsidies when their systems need improvements or expansion. Such subsidies, however, may not be forthcoming in times of economic decline, or during periods of political instability or inaction, or when the government is too far in debt or its priorities are focused on other crises – which for many governments appears to be the case more and more often.

Over time, the capacity of utilities to keep up with problems is greatly reduced. Even though big investments have been made, what do you do when they are not enough? You do what you can afford to do, not necessarily what you need to do. When this happens, maintenance is the first thing to go. It gradually becomes easier to meet lowered standards and live with the complaints until customers stop making them, which has happened in many countries around the world. It is hard to see why Canada would want to end up in such a situation.

A new water ethic for Canada has to embrace the realities of water infrastructure costs for all communities, and the need to operate, maintain and replace water system assets in a timely and affordable manner. As has already been noted, such pricing of the provision of water need not conflict with claims that water is a human right. Beyond the amounts individuals should be granted for personal use, the privilege to use water for any other purpose should be priced at levels that will ensure enough revenue to cover the cost of constructing, operating, maintaining and replacing water supply infra-structure. To be consistent with other elements of a new water ethic for Canada, the prices set for the privilege of using water in industrial and agricultural activities must include accurate and full identification and quantification of any negative externalities that may be created by providing water services if such provision results in pollution or does not respect nature's need for water or affects equitable supply of water to other communities or regions.

Subprinciple 5
Water Reuse Must Be Expanded

In many places in Canada water is simply becoming too precious to use only once before it is released downstream. Treating and reusing wastewater, where possible, has a number of advantages. It can provide a way of expanding water supply without having to construct dams, dig new wells or seed clouds in the hope of generating increased rainfall.

Reclaimed water represents a renewable supply that literally increases in volume in lockstep with population growth. Use of reclaimed water, however, has been a source of real conflict in some communities. While people don't seem to mind drinking water that has been treated after upstream use, there appears to be a stigma against drinking water reclaimed from your own sewer systems. To avoid dispute and conflict over water reuse, we will have to convince the public that reuse technology is necessary, safe and reliable.

This subprinciple will be rendered completely useless, however, if we fail to address the increasingly toxic load we are putting into water systems. Currently, even the most advanced sewage treatment systems that are still financially feasible cannot remove the residues of most of the chemicals we place in our waste water through our showers, sinks, washing machines and toilets. They cannot remove the breakdown products in the water that runs off our lawns and roadways. This must be addressed through prevention, because there can be no technological fix when all waters contain invisible, persistent, omnipresent chemical contaminants.

Subprinciple 6
Conservation Is the Foremost Imperative

Because our population is growing, there is greater pressure on water systems from agricultural and industrial use, and more water sources are unfit for other uses because we pollute them. We can avoid a water crisis, or put it off for decades while at the same time saving billions in infrastructure costs, if we make conservation a habit and concentrate fiercely on protecting the quality of our water systems. In order to make room for the future and for those who will populate it, water conservation should not be merely optional anywhere and especially not in the dry West. A new water conservation ethic, however, should not just embrace reduced human use of water supplies. It should also embrace emerging ecohydrological principles.

PRINCIPLE 5
BREAKING DOWN INSTITUTIONAL TERRITORIALITY AND JURISDICTIONAL FRAGMENTATION

The fact that we do not have an integrated vision of water management at its future and ultimate best bespeaks a problem that is so obvious that most people in the water management community have tended to ignore it. We have contradictory and often conflicting views of the ends to which we are managing water. These views are perpetuated by the atomized structure of discourse about water in Canada. Bureaucratic silos and disciplinary solitudes exist widely inside and outside of governments.

The main feature of this atomization is that those involved in discourse over water maintain their points of view by attending only those forums which support the laws or interpretations of the laws they believe are most likely to support their interests. As a result, institutional and sectoral territoriality, and jurisdictional fragmentation, continue to flourish.

While we think we are very good in North America at engineering solutions to problems of water availability and quality we have created, there is at least one overriding difficulty with the way we manage water. The trouble resides in the following facts:

~ jurisdictions often isolate themselves;
~ rules and regulations are not always followed;
~ the best mechanisms for maintaining and replacing treatment and distribution infrastructure are not always the ones that get employed; and
~ affected interests do not always share information or collaborate effectively on better water management solutions that are already available and could serve the long-term common good in a more enduring way.

These problems are only going to be exacerbated by population growth, landscape change and climatic impacts on how much water there is and when it is available. These cumulative and combined impacts are now beginning to challenge many of our own assumptions about water quality and availability in Canada.

Both federally and provincially, jurisdiction over water is most often divided between a great many individual government departments. As many as 18 different federal agencies and, depending on the province, as many as 14 provincial agencies may have jurisdiction over various aspects of water quality and management. Only Manitoba has attempted to unify some of these diverse accountabilities under a single water stewardship ministry.

The way we have atomized responsibility for managing water does not allow for any one body to fully comprehend what is actually happening to water systems in terms of the cumulative effects of population growth, landscape change and climate change. Even provincial governments, which in Canada are responsible for water management on provincial lands (not federal, First Nations or territorial lands), have not been able to keep up with the problems we have begun to create for ourselves in the West. Trapped within our own legislative, physical and operational infrastructure, the West may not be able to respond to a water crisis until it is upon us.

We cannot fix a system as fragmented as this. It has to be overhauled. One of the principles of a new Canadian water ethic has to be the restructuring, streamlining and reformation of a federal–provincial–territorial–indigenous water governance system. The first step in the process of restoring our fragmented view of water demands a change in the way we think about what elements actually constitute our water supply.

Subprinciple 1
Recognizing that Surface Water and Groundwater Are Part of the Same Supply

The degraded state of our country's groundwater resources was outlined clearly in a 2009 report by a panel led by James Bruce for the Council of Canadian Academies. The report evidences the fact that contamination of groundwater aquifers is widespread all over the country. The panel, composed of the country's best hydrologists, also pointed to long-term problems we have created for ourselves by failing to understand the link that exists between ground and surface water and denying the growing seriousness of groundwater issues in Canada.

If there is a lesson we have learned from water-scarce areas elsewhere, it is that it is just as unwise to jurisdictionally separate surface water and groundwater in management planning as it is to develop inappropriately in your headwaters. As surface water and groundwater ultimately originate from a common source, they are simply different expressions of the same supply. When surface water flows decline, it is often only a matter of time before groundwater follows. Making decisions that reflect an understanding of the direct connection between surface water and groundwater must be one of the subprinciples of Canada's next water ethic.

An example of this is the potential impact of carbon sequestration on groundwater resources. The Alberta government proposes to bury 140 million tones of CO_2 by 2050 and has invested $2-billion in demonstration projects. There is a concern, however, that CO_2 leaks may mobilize heavy metals, including arsenic and lead, in subsurface formations, leading to contamination of drinking water in excess of human-health-based limits.

Given the absence of reliable groundwater information in Canada and the lack of binding national standards for water quality, the push to accelerate carbon capture and sequestration could pose real long-term risks to our groundwater resources. In combination with widespread coalbed methane operations, we could be making things worse instead of better. In order to achieve any meaningful level of sustainability as a society, we have to improve our groundwater understanding and management.

Subprinciple 2
We Must Recognize the Value
of Continuous Monitoring

Why does good basin monitoring have to be a guerrilla activity funded, if at all, by philanthropy?
— OLIVER BRANDES

There was a time when, because of our small

population and limited ecological footprint, Canada did not have the kinds of problems most of the rest of the world faced in terms of water scarcity or water pollution. That day has passed. Because of our growth, we are now like almost everyone else in the world. We have problems with water – problems that can only be exacerbated by further growth and by climate change. In order to minimize those problems, we need to keep our finger firmly on the pulse of our country's changing hydrology.

Though it is widely held in the water management community in Canada that you can't manage what you can't measure, every time there is a federal or provincial budget cut, one of the things usually axed first is the long-term monitoring of water and the related interpretation of what the data we have already collected means. Meanwhile, we have continued to implement our economic growth imperative at a furious rate, and now, when we really need that data to make wise decisions about the future, it is not there. That has to change. Continuous, comprehensive monitoring of the state of water and our use of it, and the appropriate use of that information in decision-making, has to be recognized as one of the first principles of Canada's water ethic.

Because of climate change, the hydrology of our entire country is on the move. There is an especially crucial need for groundwater monitoring. But there is also a need for enhanced hydrological and meteorological observations and associated predictions in places like the high mountain headwaters of western Canada. Why? Because it is at these elevations that climate change impacts are expected to be felt first and to be the most pronounced in terms of their impacts on both surface water and groundwater supply. There is also an increasingly urgent need to monitor thermal pollution and rising water temperatures and their attendant effects, which often cascade quickly through aquatic ecosystems.

This is an opportunity for partnership with indigenous peoples, who have traditional methods of monitoring many aspects of the environment, including but not limited to weather patterns and changes, composition and diversity of species populations, ecosystem functioning and interrelationships, and what decision-makers refer to as "sustainable yield." A partnership-based water ethic would embrace the knowledge of community and indigenous peoples, those who know the lands and waters well, and would also rely upon this knowledge in making the best decisions regarding how we protect and use our water.

Subprinciple 3
The Concept of Integrated Water Resources Management Has To Be Informed by Different Ethics

At the United Nations Conference on Water in Mar del Plata, Argentina, in 1977, water experts from all over the world made the case that antiquated, fragmented approaches to water management and undervaluing of water had produced water policy globally that was incapable of meeting the demands of industrial society. The experts proposed, as a new ethic for determining water allocation and use, the concept of integrated water resources management. Today the technical advisory committee of the Global Water Partnership defines integrated water resources management as "a process which promotes the coordinated development and management of land, water and related resources, in order to maximize the resultant economic and social welfare in an equitable manner without compromising the sustainability of vital ecosystems."

While this concept, in combination with the emerging practice of adaptive management, has been expanded around the world, the ideals of integrated management have yet to be fully realized. Even in the most developed countries, the integrated management of land and water remains beyond reach and development continues to compromise the sustainability of vital ecosystems. The reason for this is that it is difficult to overcome the imperatives established by earlier precedents.

Adaptive management in countries such as Australia and Canada, for example, continues to frame management advances in terms of their relevance to colonial inequities established through property rights institutions such as first-in-time, first-in-right allocation protocols. These protocols often determine who is granted the status of "first" according to social or economic hierarchy rather than by historical or legal criteria. They also ignore ecological truths that will prevail in the long run as a consequence of regional hydrologic and climatic realities and trends.

While we are very good at optimizing the development potential of integrated management, we are poor at accommodating its ecosystem protection goals. We continue to lose the resilience of natural ecosystems because we remain unwilling and unable to anticipate, and unwilling to act upon, the effects of anthropogenic disturbances that radically reorder relationships within these systems in ways that diminish ultimate sustainability. Most often we look to the "good enough" solution, the solution that allows us to maintain our self-interest. We avoid saying no to ourselves, even when the failing health of vital ecosystems requires us to do so. As a result, we find ourselves now facing the turning point that decades ago defined the global water crisis widely elsewhere in the world. We are at that stage in the development of our water management institutions where the way we allocate and use water is affecting the survival of other species and the prospects of future generations of humans. Our system is not working the way we promised ourselves it would. Either we are not yet practising integrated watershed resources management in the manner required to make it work, or integrated management is not the right tool for creating true sustainability. This calls into question the most fundamental aspirations at the heart of our water management practices. The foundations of integrated water resources management have to be informed by different ethics or the concept should be abandoned.

What is required is an alignment of legislation and regulations to ensure they are based on ecological principles that support ecosystem resiliency in a changing climate. This approach, however, is at odds with the linear system of engineering which was and continues to be the main paradigm governing water management in the 20th century.

In linear system engineering, physical projects are designed to supply water, control floods, improve drainage and support transportation. Although subject to environmental assessments, these projects have tended to degrade ecological system functionality and require large fiscal and engineering resources. In a truly adaptive paradigm, "ecological engineering" would be about maintaining or restoring ecological function, recognizing its paramountcy over retaining ecosystem resiliency. Examples of this paradigm include "low impact design" in the management of rainwater to increase the use of natural drainage systems rather than engineered solutions; demand management and water conservation to reduce the need for new water supply projects; and protecting seasonal wetlands and flows in rivers and streams to sustain ecological function.

Subprinciple 4
Agricultural Policy Has To Be Tied to Water Policy

While Canadians have been distracted by water quality threats at Alberta's oil sands, the catastrophic effects of contemporary industrial-scale agricultural practices on water have been almost completely ignored. A new water ethic is needed to ensure the proper place of agriculture in Canada's economic future and to ensure that incentives exist to reduce the impact of agricultural water use and of nutrient and pesticide contamination.

A good example of where there is a need for coordinated policy is the issue of biofuels. Taking more and more land out of agricultural production and using more and more water and chemicals for non-agricultural purposes will create a vicious circle of food price increases. Not only will this make it more difficult, if not impossible, to meet future global food production needs, it will further contaminate water bodies.

Current biofuel policy is now widely seen as an excellent example of how to do the wrong thing with enthusiasm. One recent estimate argued that if we increased the fuel efficiency of North American cars by only 10 per cent, we would save the amount that is presently being invested in biofuels in the United States. Fuel production would compete less with cities, agriculture and nature for water. But that would just be a start.

The problem is not the desire to create alternative energy sources. The problem is the failure to integrate agricultural public policy, in this case with respect to biofuels, across the linked domains of water supply, land use policy, energy security and food production. Biofuel and other energy policies cannot be developed in isolation from water supply policies or agricultural water use and practices policies. If they are, expect conflict in the future over water allocation between sectors. A new Canadian water ethic will have to defuse this growing tension between water for food and water for fuel.

The first step is to create integrated or linked agricultural and water management policies. Attempts at such integration have already been initiated in Europe through the European Union's Common Agricultural Policy, or CAP. This program, initiated in the 1980s, encouraged irrigation expansion and increased water use while at the same time introducing new environmental regulations that support natural ecosystem protection.

These regulations relate to soil-conservation tillage practices, use of fertilizers and chemicals and protection of flora and fauna. The CAP reforms also demand more efficient water management measures to protect watercourses and climate change adaptation considerations. The 2005 iteration of CAP seeks to promote nothing less than a multifunctional, environmentally oriented, sustainable agriculture. The foundation for this proposed new sustainability is the dual objective of increased agricultural production and water conservation on irrigated lands.

Despite the imposition of more environmental considerations, the principal goals of the EU Common Agricultural Program have yet to be reconciled with other EU policies that seek to measurably improve water quality in river basins in member states. Progress made in Europe in the harmonization of agricultural policy and water management ideals could inspire changes in the way we do things in Canada, especially in the context of virtual water export.

Subprinciple 5
Watershed Basin Councils
Need To Be Empowered

Before we can take advantage of opportunities to expand the importance of water in our economy, we desperately need common agreement on a definition of sustainability. New understanding about how ecosystems generate and purify water will also need to become part of that foundation. Until these new ideals drive our national, provincial, territorial and indigenous water laws and policies, we are, from a public policy perspective, continuing to pretend to live in a time that no longer exists.

With so many precedents already established and so much already invested in the status quo, change is going to be difficult. This suggests that collaborative watershed basin management involving all governments and citizens is going to be needed more than ever, to address issues of trust and create forums in which concerns and potential conflicts can be forecast and the possibility of preemptive resolution outside of courts can be preserved.

But simply creating a forum for trust-building will not be enough to enable watershed management structures such as basin councils and trusts, and indigenous-led watershed management structures, to win enduring citizen and political support. It is absolutely essential to explore every avenue available for making management bodies at all levels and in all watersheds more effective in the actual final implementation of better policies and practices. There is some urgency in this if we wish to achieve water democracy.

PRINCIPLE 6
GOVERNMENTS MUST SEND
APPROPRIATE ECONOMIC SIGNALS TO EFFECT CHANGE

Governance is defined by both the presence and the absence of ethics. In the context of ethical foundations, governance is generally defined as the principles, standards and processes by which we manage our collective affairs. And on a global basis today we don't appear to be managing our collective affairs very well. Many are finding it very difficult to believe any longer in an economic system that is prepared to bring us to the brink of global freshwater, marine and terrestrial ecosystem collapse before acting on the requirement to take damage to our planetary life-support system into account when calculating pricing, taxation and real domestic product. Many others have lost or are losing faith in our economic system because it regularly takes it upon itself to plunge future generations into huge debt to perpetuate what many perceive to be a bubble economy. Others fear we will not be able to achieve the combined global poverty reduction goals and simultaneous improvements in environmental management that will enable our society to achieve any lasting level of sustainability.

Continued economic growth and poverty reduction require enormous flows of natural capital, and global ecological decline is already beginning to constrain those flows. As we cannot survive without biodiversity, clean air, fresh water and healthy oceans, Canadian water policy scholars such as the Gordon Foundation's Ralph Pentland believe that the laws of nature will have to be re-elevated above the unnatural laws of economics. Assuming we will still be operating under a market economy a quarter-century from now, the efficiencies of the free market will have to be redirected to the goals of preserving and repairing life-sustaining natural capital. A new water ethic in Canada could be the foundation of such a redirection of market power and influence.

As it is the role of government to direct the economy toward desired social ends, it is important that all governments – federal, provincial and indigenous – assert their powers. If a new water ethic is to drive a different, more sustainable future for Canada, then a series of major reforms need to be put in motion, in tandem and immediately. These reforms include:

~ higher environmental standards;
~ the strengthening of monitoring and regulatory regimes;
~ enforcement of fundamental principles such as polluter pays, full cost accounting and the precautionary principle;
~ changes in agricultural practices;
~ the development of new ways of integrating the purpose and function of urban and agricultural ecosystems; and
~ the development of the quality of cooperative effort required to get everyone working toward the same end.

These goals cannot be achieved, however, without the evolution of different kinds of economic incentives. Government has to build a new kind of track so that new breeds of free-enterprise horses can race faster around it.

Subprinciple 1
We Need To Clarify What We Mean by Water Rights

Water rights have been defined as claims by an

individual or group to use or control the use of water, which rights are recognized as legitimate by a collectivity larger than the claimants and are protected by law. A range of interests, including individuals or groups such as users, communities, corporations or states, may make various water rights claims. These claims usually include:

~ the right to use water and derive income from it;
~ the right not to use all the water one has been allocated;
~ the right to control its use and to make rules regarding water use; and
~ the right to transfer one's water rights through sale, lease, gift or inheritance.

These various kinds of rights may be grouped into two categories: rights of use, access and withdrawal; and rights of regulation, control and decision-making. Decision-making rights are often considered rights of governance. Understanding water rights in Canada demands thorough knowledge of both use rights and control rights.

Claims to water use rights in many parts of world are no longer accepted automatically as they once were. Neither are they always permanent. When populations were smaller and competition for water was less acute, it may have been sufficient to simply assert claims to water. It is sufficient no longer. Unless such claims are accepted by a collectivity larger than the claimants, they might not be considered legitimate.

The standing of relevant legitimizing institutions may also be the subject of dispute. Depending on the circumstances, the legitimizing group may be a wider users group such as an irrigation district, a village, an ethnic community, a town or city council or a provincial, cantonal or state agency. These legitimizing institutions or collectivities may be operating under competing or conflicting laws which define water rights and the rights of water users differently in different jurisdictions in the same place or region. Claims accepted and validated as legitimate by one collectivity or institution may not necessarily be accepted or recognized by another.

There is also the not insignificant matter of fundamental local values, which in some cases have been to shown to trump local laws. As many claimants have discovered to their dismay, recognition of claims over water is seldom based only on specifically defined laws and rules; it is also based on ethical principles and local cultural norms and values. While individual interests may shop for and select places with specific laws that support their water use claims, the laws that are considered valid and acceptable for a particular claim by a given interest can still be contested by the larger community, based on local values. Examples are emerging from around the world where tolerated access to water is not tantamount to a water use right. Interests such as those wishing to utilize local spring water for bottling or others wanting to use large volumes of water to extract shale gas may technically have one or another law or authority on their side, but this does not mean that outside values, common property interpretations of natural resources or options that would not be considered except in times of economic distress will translate into accepted established rights.

It is now widely held that rights to water no longer refer to a single right to access or use, but to bundles of rights that vary according to place, legal parameters and cultural values that respect the multiple ways in which humans relate to water. These bundles of rights cannot and should not be considered as static, but as subject instead to advances in ecological understanding and to shifts in social, economic and political knowledge and circumstance. In general, international discourse over water and water rights, whatever its differences, assumes the primacy of state and even international laws over religious and local laws.

Having experienced disappointments with market-based solutions, many countries are now moving toward some form of Public Trust Doctrine, a principle dating back to Roman common law, which maintains that the state must hold navigable waters and certain other defined water resource benefits as a common heritage of the people. Under this doctrine, control over water is a central pillar of sovereignty which the state cannot give up. Many observers argue that this is not just a legal principle, but a political reality in that a state that cannot meet the basic water needs of its people is not likely to endure.

The Public Trust Doctrine does not deny the economic value of water. Besides being a public good, regulating water uses can also be a source of revenue for the state. Taxes and fees for the use of water and the granting of certain decision-making rights over the use of water sources can be collected by the state to pay for the construction, operation, maintenance and replacement of water supply infrastructure. Such revenues can also be used to restore wetlands, enhance source water protection and support water-related initiatives that improve the quality of life of all citizens.

Unfortunately, Canada, particularly in the last 20 years, has been moving in a direction opposite to what international example suggests is the right way to achieve sustainability in the management of water. Observers of this shift argue that we have to change three things simultaneously if we are to avoid the kinds of problems that exist elsewhere with respect to equitable water availability and reliable quality.

The first change we need is in the practice of democracy. Currently governments are being heavily influenced by corporations and other established economic interests and are not responding adequately to citizen input.

The second change that is required is the immediate movement toward an "ecological economics" in which the true cost of damage to the planetary commons is calculated into the cost of the goods and services we provide to one another.

The third is a shift in our cultural values.

At present we operate under a principle of utility that asserts that actions are right provided they promote the greatest happiness for the greatest number of people. Majority interests are expected to trump minority rights. Further, we have little common vision of what happiness means or to what ends we are advancing through our commitment to relentless growth and ever greater prosperity. Happiness in this context is also confined to what pleases people, not the systems that make life possible for those people. Critics of the utility principle argue that we are too busy maximizing our own self-interest to meet the moral obligation to consider and meet the needs of a broader range of others.

At present the calculation of broader utility is often considered too complicated to undertake; that living up to the moral ideal of making that calculation is beyond our reach. As decline of global life systems accelerates, however, who defines utility – and even the validity of the principle itself – is likely to be widely challenged. If we wish to survive as a nation over the long term, we should shift our view now from anthropocentrism to an interconnected worldview that recognizes the importance of our expanded relations with the other living things and life systems with which we share Canada.

Subprinciple 2
We Need To Accept the Limits of Markets

A new water ethic in Canada would admit that markets are not the appropriate tool for effective long-term management of water. This should not be taken as a condemnation of the free-enterprise system. The fact is, however, that some things possess value that lies outside the capacity of markets to properly represent. Water is one of those things. Markets have limited application to broader water management concerns because they were not created to address problems of social, environmental, cultural, intergenerational or interspecies equity. Markets are an economic tool that can address, often crudely as with most blunt instruments, some economic issues. Better pricing and more-open markets will serve to assign water a higher economic value in its economic functions. While it is true that better pricing and more open markets do generate healthy competition that will discourage wasteful and unproductive uses, markets alone cannot solve the real problem we face. The real problem we face, as Sandra Postel so eloquently argues, is that we lack a set of principles – laws, policies, guidelines; in essence a management framework – that stops us from chipping away at natural systems until there is nothing left of their life-sustaining functions, which the marketplace fails to value adequately, if it values them at all.

As we have seen recently, and likely will see again, markets are excellent servants but poor masters. Water markets will remain imperfect tools until they focus as much on sustainability and intergenerational equity as they do on short-term profit. We have to be particularly wary of unpriced externalities and imperfect information. In order to produce sustainable results, markets have to be directed toward appropriate ends by thoughtful public policy. Until such a framework is developed and made legally enforceable, ethical issues associated with who presently can use water in what volumes and for what purposes must be reviewed.

At present we have the cart before the horse in the water market debate in Canada. What we need before we develop further reliance on new economic instruments is a new water ethic, one that provides a guide to right conduct in the face of the difficult decisions we need to make that impact natural systems we do not and cannot fully understand. We need to develop that ethic before we create markets. If we do not, then the markets that come into existence will do more damage than good and will stand in the way of creating more integrated water sources management practices in the future.

Specifically, if we could:

~ demonstrate that First Nations' needs and rights have been addressed;
~ satisfactorily define the water pricing and conservation measures that will be put in place to

free up more water for minimum human use and other purposes now and in the future;

~ describe the actions that in tandem will be taken to measurably reduce eutrophication and other water quality impacts of agricultural practices;

~ develop and codify exactly the practices that will be put in place to assure adequate environmental flows; and

~ illustrate the government structure that will provide appropriate, effective and timely oversight of the above and all market transactions,

then we might have our house in order enough to be able to look at utility water markets if need still warrants. Let us not fool ourselves, though; we are not there yet.

Subprinciple 3
We Must Recognize the Link
between Water and Energy

Most Canadians have yet to make the link between water use and energy costs. It takes a lot of water to produce energy and a lot of energy to move water. Water is heavy. It takes a great deal of energy to abstract, treat, distribute and re-treat it for further use. Some municipalities spend up to 60 per cent of their energy budget moving water to where it is needed when it is needed.

While most Canadians wouldn't think of leaving a light on when they leave a room, they don't think about water conservation. They don't think about the (most often) indigenous communities that live at the other end of the transmission line, alongside territories flooded and eroding as a result of hydroelectric generating stations that have dammed up rivers.

There is another direct link between water and energy. Global energy consumption will continue to rise, increasing by perhaps as much as 50 per cent by 2030. This will put the energy sector into greater competition with other water users, which will likely impact regional energy reliability and supply. The requirement for new energy sources such as coalbed methane and shale gas will also exacerbate water overuse and further increase tensions over water security. Thus it becomes crucial to increase the efficiency of water use in energy production. Huge growth is also projected in unconventional biofuels and substitutions. That said, we should not be growing fuel where we should be growing food.

The consequences of our inability to manage the water/energy nexus could be grave. Until our thinking about water and energy can be integrated, sustainability will continue to elude us.

Saving water and saving energy are the same thing. If you save one, you usually save the other. Leaving your tap run for five minutes costs the same as letting a 60-watt light bulb burn for 14 hours. And that calculation does not account for the downstream cost of greenhouse gas emissions. With a new Canadian water ethic, we commit to identifying and building on the cost-saving and environmental-impact-reducing link between water and energy rather than continually searching for new sources of energy and electricity generation.

Subprinciple 4
Opportunity Resides In New
Perspectives on Water

A new water ethic would allow Canadians to re-think the value of what we have, in the broader context of a changing world. Such thinking

– tied to new incentives – would allow Canada to protect its prosperity while at the same time contributing to the well-being of others. Globally the divide is already growing between freshwater haves and have-nots. As Steven Solomon notes in his book *Water: The Epic Struggle for Wealth, Power, and Civilization*, this explosive fault line between those who have enough water and those who do not is likely to widen across the entire political, social and economic landscape of the 21st century. India is expected to experience a 50 per cent water shortfall by 2030. The water shortfall in China will be 25 per cent by 2030. The gap between water haves and have-nots will widen between those who control upriver water flows and their downstream neighbours who do not receive all the water they need for factories and cities. The gap will widen even more between nations that have sufficient water supplies to grow their own food and those that do not. Currently, 85 per cent of the world's 525 million farms are less than five acres in size. We are, at the very minimum, faced with the prospect of having to produce twice as much food with 10 per cent less water if we are to feed the population we are expected to have in 2050, only 40 years hence.

But water availability will not just affect food production. The amount of water available to a given nation will determine its industrial capacity and the quality of life its citizens enjoy as a result of nature receiving the water it needs to make places be worth living in. Prosperous countries in the future will be those that have enough water for food, for cities, for industry and for nature.

Increasingly, the response to global water scarcity will be defined not by direct transfers of liquid water between regions and countries, but by how much water is traded among nations in the form of water embodied in food and other products that require considerable water for their production.

As of 2000, about 1000 cubic kilometres of water was being traded from nation to nation in the form of food. We have yet to calculate the relative virtual water costs and benefits of exporting and importing trade goods, but it will soon be necessary to do so. Models predict that by 2050 some 53 per cent of the population of the world will be facing one form or another of water scarcity.

If this happens, countries that need to make up for inadequate water supply by importing water virtually as food will require a global virtual transfer of 7500 cubic kilometres per year. Provided we can get our own house in order with respect to the management of water, this growth in virtual water trade internationally could be of great importance to Canada economically. Some experts have predicted that as a result of this trade, agriculture will ultimately become even more important to our economy than oil and gas. It could also, however, exacerbate problems of already threatened water bodies, and could increase even further the levels of domestic competition for water use.

Global warming is lining up to have an explosive impact on the reliability of national and regional water supplies. A new world order is about to emerge from the collision between population and economic growth and our planet's rapidly changing hydrology.

Canada's future does not have to reside in becoming a global fossil-fuel energy superpower.

Our future could just as easily lie in the export of products that other parts of the world need but cannot produce due to lack of water. We can only be successful, however, if our water management is founded on the development of sustainable, scaled-to-situation water supply techniques that make more productive use of available water supplies while at the same time protecting our ecosystems and ways of life.

PRINCIPLE 7
WE CANNOT SUCCEED WITHOUT POLITICAL LEADERSHIP

We face a vacuum in domestic and international water leadership. New forms of hydro-diplomacy are desperately needed. Everyone knows what the problem is but political will, financial resources and good governance are widely lacking.

Leaders and policy-makers are inundated by "legislative congestion," but the fact remains that inactivity in the face of a growing global water crisis is unconscionable. Future generations will drink the very same water we drink. There is, therefore, huge urgency in creating the political will to address the root causes of the global water crisis.

International example demonstrates that it is not enough just to collaborate on the subject of possible public policy evolution and changes in practice. Talk generated within collaborative frameworks, such as those created by watershed basin councils or other water use management structures, has to be translated into action if it is going to mean anything over the long term. We have to acknowledge the substantial gap that presently exists between promise and practice. We have to acknowledge also that the only way to fill that gap is through leadership provided by the most senior levels of government.

Subprinciple 1
It Is a Good Time To Create a New Vision

It is to our federal, provincial, territorial and in-digenous leaders that the responsibility for cre-ating a new water ethic in Canada must fall, for they are the only ones with the power to make the sweeping changes necessary to the political and legal structures that will make reform pos-sible. There is opportunity in acting now. As

Bill Lahey, a law professor and former deputy minister of environment and labour in Nova Scotia recently pointed out, a new Canadian water ethic may be just what is needed to bring about widespread change in the way we manage and protect water, not just in Nova Scotia but everywhere in Canada. Effective policy change, he explained, needs an organizing principle or ethic around which the people and the politicians that represent them can rally. By way of demonstrating the power of such an ethic, Lahey cited the healthcare debate that took place in Canada during the 1960s, when the ethic of free care for everyone emerged as the driving principle in the reform of our country's healthcare system. Lahey noted that the ethic at the heart of this principle remained strong enough, 30 years later, to repel three attacks on it by Alberta Premier Ralph Klein, who, throughout his long tenure, advocated repeatedly for private healthcare. We need Canadians to get behind a new water ethic in the same way they got behind universal healthcare.

Lahey further argued that because there is less debate about water than about many other resources, the move to create a new water ethic could enable a good many related environmental problems to be addressed simultaneously en route to better water management. The affirmation of a new water ethic may also be a means of ultimately achieving greater capacity to adapt to climate change.

Subprinciple 2
Climate Change Has Made Water Policy Reform an Urgent Priority

Climate security equals water security.
— DR. JAMES BRUCE

It has become increasingly clear that we did not have any real idea what we were signing up for when our government decided for us as a nation that it would be cheaper and less inconvenient to adapt to climate change than to address it. Observing how glibly we toss the notion of adaptation around, one would think that what we are facing in the future are just a few simple adjustments – like getting used to daylight saving time or metric measure or new rules regarding cell phone use while driving. Recent research outcomes related to Canada's rapidly changing hydrology make it clear that adaptation is going to mean much more than that. The very fact that we could not change our behaviours to mitigate or lessen our reliance on fossil fuels shows how tenuous our assertion is that we can change our behaviours and adapt to a new world massively impacted by climate change.

We acquiesced to adaptation. Choosing this path without thinking of the consequences of the climate change threat implies a willingness to deal somehow with tens of millions of environmental refugees, conflicts at home and abroad over water supplies, enormous costs associated with protecting coastal cities from rising sea levels, and hugely expensive repairs of damage to our cities caused by more frequent and intense rain, snow, ice storms and floods.

By choosing to adapt rather than act on the core of the climate change problem, we are implicitly agreeing to accept the loss of the Canadian Arctic as we know it and that we will somehow manage through 45°C summer temperatures on the prairies and absorb the enormous economic costs associated with deep and prolonged drought that could lead to food shortages. Because we are choosing to adapt rather than respond to the climate threat, we have accepted that we will live with more frequent wildfires, an increase in invasive plant and animal species, the likelihood of new diseases – all resulting in a lower quality of life for ourselves and our children.

The trajectory of climate change is set and adaptation is essential. But this is only part of the problem. We are not just accepting on faith that we can adapt to the partially characterized future climate circumstances which our governments have determined on our behalf will be acceptable to us as a consequence of inaction. We are also affected by cuts in funding to the very research that will identify for us what those future conditions might actually be like.

One of Canada's most renowned scientists, Dr. James Bruce, has pointed out that climate change projections by the Intergovernmental Panel on Climate Change are likely too cautious and that some effects are already occurring faster than expected. Despite this, he said, global emissions continue to rise. At the time of this writing, we are facing a "business as usual" climate change scenario globally.

Total global emissions, Dr. Bruce explained, are now 41 per cent above 1990 levels. As a result, impacts on the Arctic are becoming obvious: glaciers are visibly receding; ice on Canadian lakes and rivers is disappearing; and extreme weather events are becoming more common. Dr. Bruce observed that if the changes that have taken place over the past 40 years continue, Canada should expect to experience significant climate-related impacts on its water supplies. He concluded by pointing out that in the Canadian context, climate security equals water security. Canadians should be taking climate change seriously. The fact that our country's hydrology is on the move makes water policy reform in Canada an urgent priority and the creation of a new water ethic essential to our future.

Subprinciple 3
We Have Viable, Interesting Options

There are at least three potential avenues of reform. We can revitalize the current system by activating unexercised jurisdiction and harmonizing federal, provincial, territorial, indigenous and municipal oversight with respect to the management of our water sources. Revitalization of the existing system will require improved monitoring, forecasting and prediction tied to better enforcement of existing laws. It will also require new legislation and regulations that protect water quality and recognize nature's need for water.

Alternatively, water policy reform in Canada could emerge from the example of others. One immediately wonders if it might not be worthwhile considering implementing programs in Canada similar to those undertaken by the European Union and its member states by means of the Water Framework Directive. Though it is not perfect, this policy instrument enables the EU to define water quality standards and parameters of aquatic ecosystem health, and individual nations are then charged with meeting those standards by whatever means they feel will work best in local circumstances.

Certainly, if the EU – with its 27 member states and population of 500 million people speaking 23 official languages and occupying a territory of 4,324,782 square kilometres – can create a continental water framework, it is conceivable that a single country with only 33 million people speaking only two official national languages spread through 10 provinces and three territories should be able to do something comparable even though that single country is more than twice the size geographically: 9,984,670 square kilometres, though encompassing what are really only five major watersheds. Without question we have the capacity to create a similar groundswell of change. All we have to do is want to.

The European Declaration for a New Water Culture provides four broad categories for ethical action in water management. The first is "water for life," both human and non-human. This is interesting in that it places water for people and water for nature on equal footing as the foundation of a new European water ethic, whereas our water ethic in North America does not grant water to nature until all human needs have been met. No matter what policy instruments we ultimately employ, the institutional challenge of freeing more water for natural ecosystem function demands we do more than simply insist that nature compete with past precedents in water allocation.

The Declaration also stands on the foundation of a citizen-based water ethic that aims to ensure that water becomes an instrument for maintaining adequate supply and sanitation, not just for health but for well-being, social cohesion, social capital and capacity-building. The Declaration further recognizes the "water industry" as an essential element in economic growth, though this is a third level of priority. Unlike in Canada and the US, it is considered unethical under the terms and conditions of the European Water Framework Directive to allow business concerns to interfere with water for life.

Finally, the Declaration takes a firm ethical stance against crimes against water, which include destructive withdrawal practices, toxic spills and other actions that threaten the planet's precious and irreplaceable water systems. This is radically different from the ethic that presently informs water management decisions in North America, where, in the absence of adherence to the precautionary principle, the burden of proving why particular water allocations or operational practices threaten the sustainability of water systems rests entirely upon those who would oppose them.

A third avenue of reform might be to allow regions to reform water policy on a large-scale watershed basis. The premiers of the western provinces and northern territories have created the Western Water Stewardship Council, which aims to resolve potential conflicts in the management of all the river systems that have their origins in Canada's western mountains. Perhaps something similar might emerge in the St. Lawrence and Great Lakes areas and in Atlantic Canada through the newly formed Council of the Federation, which includes representation of first ministers from all the provinces and territories as well as the federal government. Because it also includes First Nations, perhaps the Northwest Territories' recently ratified Northern Voices, Northern Waters strategy might be the best model for a more integrated water policy design process in Canada.

Unlike so many other places in the world, Canada still has room to move in how it manages water. If we can equitably and fairly balance the water availability and quality needs of all people and nature, agriculture and industry, everything else we need to do to become sustainable, including addressing climate change, may very well fall into line. With a new water ethic in place we could become a sustainable society. Then we really will be leaders, with something new and useful to share with the rest of the world. If this is what we desire, however, we need to get moving while the room to move is still there.

Subprinciple 4
We Urgently Need a New Relationship among the Provinces, Territories, Indigenous Peoples and the Federal Government Concerning Water

As the divide deepens between those with sufficient water and those without, the politics of water scarcity will become increasingly pivotal in shaping the world order of the 21st century. To survive and prosper in this environmentally dangerous and politically unstable time, we have to get our water house in order. To even begin to do this, we need a new water ethic.

Implementing a partnership ethic for the management of water in Canada will not be easy. Constructing the future will entail reusing stones from the edifice we need to tear down. Despite efforts to advance in the direction of integrated water management and governance innovations such as watershed basin authorities and councils, the growth imperative of a free-market economy remains the dominant natural resources management ethic in almost every province and territory in the country.

While efforts are being made to create a green economy based on variations of free-market principles, Canada's brand of capitalism continues to undercut its own sustainability by using nature faster than nature can restore itself or be restored. Major systems are already becoming degraded. In the meantime, the management of these systems is becoming more complicated and difficult because ecosystems are losing stability and will likely continue to do so as temperatures rise. We are faced with little choice. If we want to preserve the fundamental freedoms that form the foundation of our democracy, we have to modify our economic systems to make them compatible with sustainability and inter-generational equity.

What we know about the ecological cum economic foundations of life on this planet suggests that some form of expanded partnership ethic will be necessary if we want to achieve any meaningful level of long-term sustainability. This is not going to be easy to sell, however. It is not just the precedents and habits of our economic system that argue against the emergence of a partnership ethic.

The property rights movement and libertarian forces in many parts of Canada are very strong. The creation and protection of private property and the right to profit maximization form the foundation of our country's laws and are fundamental to the egocentric ethic that over the last century has elevated the protection of these rights to the centre of government and institutional purpose. To these interests the partnership-with-water ethic will be anathema. The backlash against environmentalism and what these interests consider to be ecocentrism is likely to be unreasonable, adversarial and continuous. Unfortunately, if we don't want to end up like many other countries in the world in terms of water woes, we have to face the problems we have created for ourselves. Because we have not attended to matters related to water policy in this country for more than two decades, it will take a great deal of collaboration, patience and uncommon courage and vision to lead Canada in the direction of a sustainable future

Subprinciple 5
We Need To Cultivate Leadership Now

We have a messy situation on our hands. Water is non-replaceable, and for this reason if no other, we have come to the realization that we should treat water very differently than things we have labelled "resources." If we want to achieve sustainability, we need a new water ethic, new governance and new results. It won't be easy and it won't always work on the first try, but if we all want to survive on this planet, we have little choice but to recognize some sort of partnership with water as a beginning, as something in which we can invest hope. Determining what is sustainable with respect to the privilege of using water in the context of the needs of human and non-human communities is going to have to be renegotiated. The difficult task that confronts us resides in demonstrating that individual, community or corporate ownership of property are not necessarily inconsistent with a partnership ethic or with a soft-path approach to water management.

It will take the highest order of statesmanship by all leaders in Canada to create the broad-based, non-partisan political support required for bringing a new Canadian water ethic into being. In order to prepare ourselves for the future, Canadians should begin cultivating that leadership now.

Notes

1   *114957 Canada Ltée (Spraytech, Société d'arrosage) v.*
    Hudson (Town), [2001] 2 S.C.R. 241. Available online at
    http://is.gd/I5OE9E (accessed 2011-06-15).

2   Hoel, D.G., et al. *J Natl Cancer Inst 84*(5) (1992-03-04):
    313–320.

3   Nederlof, K.P., et al. *MMWR 39*(4) (1990-12-01): 9–17.

4   Carlsen, E., et al. *Br Med J 305* (1992-09-12): 609–613.

Bookshelf

Brown, Peter G. "Are There Any Natural Resources?" In Brown and Schmidt, *Water Ethics*, as c. 19: 203–220.

Brown, Peter G., and Jeremy J. Schmidt, eds. *Water Ethics: Foundational Readings for Students and Professionals.* Washington, DC: Island Press, 2010.

Bruce, James B., et al. "The Sustainable Management of Groundwater in Canada." Report of the Expert Panel on Groundwater. Ottawa: Council of Canadian Academies, 2009. Available online (PDF) at http://is.gd/mlHNjC (accessed 2011-05-20).

Carlsen, E., et al. "Evidence for Decreasing Quality of Semen during Past 50 Years." *British Medical Journal 305* (1992-09-12): 609–613.

de Loë, R.C. "Toward a Canadian National Water Strategy." Report Prepared for the Canadian Water Resources Assn. Guelph, Ont.: Rob de Loë Consulting Services, 2008. Available online at www.cwra.org/Resource/assets/CNWS_Report_Final_2008_06_18.pdf (accessed 2011-05-18).

Gleick, Peter H. *Bottled & Sold: The Story Behind Our Obsession with Bottled Water.* Washington, DC: Island Press, 2010.

Hoel, David G., et al. "Trends in Cancer Mortality in 15 Industrialized Countries 1969–1986." *Journal of the National Cancer Institute 84*, no. 5 (1992-03-04): 313–320.

Merchant, Carolyn. "Fish First! The Changing Ethics of Ecosystem Management." In Brown and Schmidt, *Water Ethics*, as c. 21: 227–240.

Nederlof, Kees P., et al. "Ectopic Pregnancy Surveillance, United States, 1970–1987." *Morbidity & Mortality Weekly Reporter 39*, no. 4 (1990-12-01): 9–17.

New Water Culture Foundation. *European Declaration for a New Water Culture*. Zaragoza: Fundación Nueva Cultura del Agua, 2005.

Northwest Territories. *Northern Voices, Northern Waters: Towards a Water Resources Management Strategy for the NWT*. Yellowknife: Environment and Natural Resources, Government of the Northwest Territories, 2008.

Phare, Merrell-Ann S. *Denying the Source: The Crisis of First Nations Water Rights*. Calgary: Rocky Mountain Books, 2009.

Postel, Sandra. "The Missing Piece: A Water Ethic." In Brown and Schmidt, *Water Ethics*, as c. 20: 221–226.

Pradhan, Rajendra, and Ruth Meinzen-Dick. "Which Rights Are Right? Water Rights, Culture, and Underlying Values." In Brown and Schmidt, *Water Ethics*, as c. 5: 39–58.

Sandford, Robert W. *Restoring the Flow: Confronting the World's Water Woes*. Calgary: Rocky Mountain Books, 2009.

———. *Water, Weather and the Mountain West*. Calgary: Rocky Mountain Books, 2007.

Schmidt, Jeremy. "Water Ethics and Water Management." In Brown and Schmidt, *Water Ethics*, as c. 1: 3–16.

Smith, Adam. *The Wealth of Nations*. London: J.M. Dent, 1977. First published in 1776 as *An Inquiry into the Nature and Causes of the Wealth of Nations*.

Solomon, Steven. *Water: The Epic Struggle for Wealth, Power, and Civilization*. New York: Harper, 2010.

Other Titles in this Series

THE INSATIABLE BARK BEETLE

Dr. Reese Halter

ISBN 978-1-926855-66-0

THE INCOMPARABLE HONEYBEE

and the Economics of Pollination
Revised & Updated

Dr. Reese Halter

ISBN 978-1-926855-64-6

BECOMING WATER

Glaciers in a Warming World

Mike Demuth

ISBN 978-1-926855-72-1

THE BEAVER MANIFESTO

Glynnis Hood

ISBN 978-1-926855-58-5

THE GRIZZLY MANIFESTO

In Defence of the Great Bear

Jeff Gailus

ISBN 978-1-897522-83-7

DENYING THE SOURCE

The Crisis of First Nations Water Rights

Merrell-Ann S. Phare

ISBN 978-1-897522-61-5

THE WEEKENDER EFFECT

Hyperdevelopment in Mountain Towns

Robert William Sandford

ISBN 978-1-897522-10-3

RMB saved the following resources by printing the pages of this book on chlorine-free paper made with 100% post-consumer waste:

Trees · 10, fully grown

Water · 4,537 gallons

Solid Waste · 275 pounds

Greenhouse Gases · 942 pounds

Calculations based on research by Environmental Defense and the Paper Task Force. Manufactured at Friesens Corporation.